THE
DEE BRESTIN
SERIES

A WOMAN
OF
Beauty

David C Cook®
transforming lives together

The Dee Brestin Series
From David C Cook
BOOKS
The Friendships of Women

BIBLE STUDY GUIDES

A WOMAN OF LOVE
Using Our Gift for Intimacy (Ruth)

A WOMAN OF FAITH
Overcoming the World's Influences
(Esther)

A WOMAN OF PURPOSE
Walking with the Savior (Luke)

A WOMAN OF WORSHIP
Praying with Power (10 Psalms with a
music CD)

A WOMAN OF MODERATION
Breaking the Chains of Poor Eating
Habits (Topical)

A WOMAN OF CONTENTMENT
Insight into Life's Sorrows
(Ecclesiastes)

A WOMAN OF BEAUTY
Becoming More Like Jesus
(1, 2, 3 John)

A WOMAN OF WISDOM
God's Practical Advice for Living
(Proverbs)

THE FRIENDSHIPS OF WOMEN
BIBLE STUDY GUIDE correlates
with THE FRIENDSHIPS OF
WOMEN

A WOMAN OF BEAUTY
Published by David C Cook
4050 Lee Vance View
Colorado Springs, CO 80918 U.S.A.

David C Cook Distribution Canada
55 Woodslee Avenue, Paris, Ontario, Canada N3L 3E5

David C Cook U.K., Kingsway Communications
Eastbourne, East Sussex BN23 6NT, England

The graphic circle C logo is a registered trademark of David C Cook.

All Scripture quotations, unless otherwise noted, are taken from the Holy Bible, New International Version®. NIV®. Copyright ©
1973, 1978, 1984 by International Bible Society. Used by permission of Zondervan. All rights reserved. Scripture quotations marked
MSG are taken from THE MESSAGE. Copyright © by Eugene Peterson 1993, 1994, 1995, 1996, 2000, 2001, 2002. Used by permission
of NavPress Publishing Group. Scripture quotations marked PH are taken from J.B. Phillips: The New Testament in Modern
English, revised editions © J.B. Phillips, 1958, 1960, 1972, permission of Macmillan Publishing Co. and Collins Publishers. Scripture
quotations marked KJV are taken from the King James Version of the Bible. Scripture quotations marked NKJV are taken from the
New King James Version. Copyright © 1982 by Thomas Nelson, Inc. Used by permission. All rights reserved. Scripture quotations
marked NLT are taken from the Holy Bible, New Living Translation, Copyright © 1996. Used by permission of Tyndale House
Publishers, Inc., Wheaton, Illinois, 60189. All rights reserved. Scripture quotations marked NASB are taken from the New American
Standard Bible. © Copyright 1960, 1962,1963, 1968, 1971, 1972, 1973, 1975, 1977 by The Lockman foundation. Used by permission.
Scripture quotations marked AMP are taken from The Amplified Bible. Copyright ©v 1954, 1958,1962, 1964, 1965, 1987 by The
Lockman Foundation. Used by permission. Scripture quotations marked ESV are taken from The Holy Bible,English Standard
Version, Copyright © 2000; 2001 by Crossway Bibles, a division of Good News Publishers. Used by permission. All rights reserved.

ISBN 978-0-7814-4451-4
eISBN 978-1-4347-0407-8

Interior Design: Nancy L. Haskins
Cover Design: Greg Jackson, Thinkpen Design, llc
Cover Photo: 2006 ©BigStockPhoto

Printed in the United States of America
First Edition 2006

8 9 10 11 12 13

060514

Contents

To Eunice Arant,

whose radiance gives hope, not only to the women
in the Omaha jails, but also to all who meet her.

Introduction

Beauty secrets. Women's magazines are full of them. Models and movie stars whisper to eager readers how they got their flawless complexions, slim figures, and full lips.

However, even if we capture this beauty, it is only for a moment. For, as God tells us, outward "beauty is fleeting" (Prov. 31:30). It is vanity, which means "something passing swiftly away."

But there is a kind of beauty that will never fade, that is precious in the sight of God. And, amazingly, those beauty secrets are found in the letters of John. John tells us how to grow in beauty, so that one day "we may have confidence and not be ashamed before Him at His coming" (1 John 2:28 NKJV).

Have the first lesson done before the first discussion time. But if you have just received this guide, do the best you can in group, and then prepare the following lessons ahead of time. (If the whole group just received their guides, read the text aloud and discuss only the questions in bold.)

In the back of this guide are hymns and praise choruses for you to begin each day in worship. Worship can open the heart for God's Spirit to slip truths in.

You will also find your memory verses at the back in case you want to cut the page out and post it somewhere or simply refer to it for review.

The Scripture study is divided into five days, for five personal quiet times with the Lord.

Leaders will find helps in the back.

One

What Makes a Woman Beautiful?

Esther 1—2; 1 Peter 3:1–6; Psalm 45, and excerpts from the Old Testament

Man has always looked on the outward appearance. Pick up any glossy women's magazine and estimate how much space is given to outer beauty versus the space given to character. We are surrounded by these values, and we must fight not to allow, as J. B. Phillips' paraphrase of Romans 12:1 puts it, "the world around [us] squeeze [us] into its own mold."

Before we begin the letters of John to discover God's beauty secrets, we need to first consider how God views beauty. Physical beauty is not without value, but it will fade, and there is a beauty that will never fade.

WARMUP

Each woman should share her name, a little about herself, and why she came to this study. Throw out some standards of beauty from women's magazines. How do they make you feel?

DAY I

Man Looks on the Outward Appearance

God's Word can be a wake-up call. There is much in the book of Esther that can help us see the folly of this world's standards. If we miss the enormous satire in the book of Esther, we miss the point. Too often we remember it only as it was told to us as children—the edited version, the "Veggie Tales" version. But that version is distorted, misses the satire, and misses much of the point God is making. It is important to understand that the values in ancient Persia were very worldly, yet amazingly similar to our twenty-first-century values. Women were valued primarily for their outward beauty, youth, and sexual allure. A look at the book of Esther helps us understand that we are under the very same pressure that women in the days of ancient Persia faced.

So often, outside of the influence of Christ, women are treated as second-class citizens and as sex objects, causing them to be used and abused. Consequently, it is hard for women who live in this world and are surrounded by its values not to begin to measure themselves by the world's standards, elevating physical beauty above kindness, integrity, and all the aspects of character that are so precious to God.

In chapter 2 of Esther we learn about a "beauty" contest that is taking place to choose the new queen of Persia. As part of this contest, King Xerxes (or your translation may say Ahasuerus) slept with a different virgin each night for months, possibly even years. These were probably very young girls who had been taken from 127 separate provinces because of their beauty. Though they may have been told it was an honor to be chosen—it was not.

In Japan, beautiful little girls were often "chosen" to be trained to be geishas, women who learned to please men with dance, tea ceremonies, and sexual pleasure. Geishas were known as high-class mistresses. In Arthur Golden's *Memoirs of a Geisha,* Chiyo is a young girl "chosen" for training. As she anticipates meeting the first time with her trainer, she watches her father load baskets of fish into a horse-drawn wagon.

> *I climbed up on the wagon to watch. Mostly the fish stared out with glassy eyes, but every so often one would move its mouth, which seemed to me like a little scream. I tried to reassure them by saying:*
>
> *"You're going to the town of Senzuru, little fishies! Everything will be okay."*
> *I didn't see what good it would be to tell them the truth.* (Random House, 1997, p. 24)

Likewise, hundreds, perhaps thousands of young virgins were caught in the immoral net of Xerxes' beauty contest and "trained" for his pleasure.

The book of Esther opens with a six month party as Xerxes tries to impress military leaders with his wealth, power, and voluptuous wife. The party closes with seven days of intense drinking.

Read Esther 1

1. Try to pick up on the satire in this chapter, where the Lord is "laughing" at Xerxes and his self-importance, his distorted values, and his foiled plan. Write down everything you see.

2. What did Xerxes demand of his "beautiful" wife, and why do you think this might have been an abuse to her?

After Vashti is banished (or some say beheaded) for her "disobedience," a beauty contest for the new Queen of Persia begins. Again, this is written satirically, for God in heaven is watching and weeping at man's abuse of women (this can be studied in depth in *A Woman of Faith*). In each of Xerxes' 127 provinces, a quest begins for the next woman to take the queen's place and beautiful young virgins are "taken" (the implication is that force was used). The phrase "please the king" has a strong sexual connotation, for it is the same word Samson used when he lusted after the Philistine woman in Judges 14, "Get her for me for she pleases me!"

Read Esther 2:1–18 again, watching for the satire.

3. Describe the plan and the standards to find the new queen in Esther 2:1–4.

4. Do you think these standards would lead to a queen that could rule her people well? Explain.

5. Describe the beauty treatments each girl had to undergo before her night with the king.

6. When did the girl go to the king and when did she return? Why do you think she went to live with the concubines instead of back with the virgins?

God allows men to make immoral choices, yet nothing slips between His fingers. There is a strong sense in the Hebrew that He was with Esther as she endured this abuse. Clearly, God's Spirit did not engineer this contest, for God is not the author of evil. Yet He allows sin to reign for a time. He is a master of bringing beauty out of ashes (Isa. 61:3). If you were a victim of sexual abuse, know that God saw, God wept, and God can bring beauty out of ashes.

Begin memorizing 1 John 1:5 (memory verses are also in the back if you want to tear out the page for your mirror, kitchen sink, etc.):

> *This is the message we have heard from him and declare to you: God is light; in him there is no darkness at all.*

DAY 2

God Looks on the Heart

Physical beauty has always played a part in the choice of leaders, for man looks on the outward appearance. Before the age of television, it was possible to elect a homely man like Abraham Lincoln, but now that the world can see the candidates, a man who looks like a movie star (or is a movie star) has a much better chance of getting elected. In *Amusing Ourselves to Death*, Neil Postman writes: "we may have reached the point where cosmetics has replaced ideology as the field of expertise over which a politician must have competent control" (Penguin Books, 1986, p. 4).

Even we, as believers, value people on the basis of their outward appearance. Though Eliab showed himself to be a proud and envious man, when the prophet Samuel saw him and how tall and handsome he was, Samuel thought, "Surely the LORD's anointed stands here before the LORD" (1 Sam. 16:6).

7. What does God tell Samuel in 1 Samuel 16:7?

8. According to Isaiah 53:2, what do you learn about the physical appearance of Jesus?

9. The book of Proverbs has warnings to young men about women who are physically beautiful. What do the following passages tell you about physical beauty versus character?

   A. Proverbs 6:23–26

   B. Proverbs 11:22

   C. Proverbs 31:10–12

10. The Pharisees were impressive to many. Yet what did Jesus see and articulate in Matthew 23:27?

11. In contrast, what does Jesus say about Mary of Bethany, who is being severely criticized for anointing Him with perfume (Matt. 26:6–13)?

12. Read 1 Peter 3:1–6.

   A. What, according to verses 1–2, may make husbands who do not obey the Word sit up and take notice?

   B. How does the Lord describe true beauty according to verses 3–4?

   C. Read 1 Peter 3:3–4 again in the *Amplified Bible*:

   Let not yours be the [merely] external adorning with [elaborate] interweaving and knotting of the hair, the wearing of jewelry, or changes of clothes; But let it be the inward adorning and beauty of the hidden person of the heart, with the incorruptible and unfading charm of a gentle and peaceful spirit, which [is not anxious or wrought up, but] is very precious in the sight of God.

   Do you gain any new insights from this version?

It isn't that physical beauty is not a gift or that we shouldn't care about our outward appearance. Clearly the virtuous woman of Proverbs 31 dressed well. But our world is flying upside down. The inner person simply is not valued, the heart is not kept clean, and gentleness and kindness are vastly underrated. How vital it is that we not be conformed to the world, but transformed by the Word of God.

   D. How did the holy women of old make themselves beautiful? (v. 5)

First Peter 3:6 refers to the example of how Sara called Abraham lord. "Do not give way to fear" is another way of saying "put your hope in God." (This passage can be studied in depth in *A Woman of Confidence*.)

   E. In your life, where is God calling you to put your hope in Him rather than give way to fear?

13. A contrast to the beauty that is precious in God's sight is found in the "women of Zion" in Isaiah 3:16–24. How does the prophet Isaiah warn them?

14. What is God impressing on your heart from today's lesson?

Continue memorizing 1 John 1:5:

This is the message we have heard from him and declare to you: God is light; in him there is no darkness at all.

DAY 3

Unworthy, but Beautiful

There are three love stories in the Old Testament that have a deeper meaning than simple earthly romance. In each, the bride represents you and me as believers, and the bridegroom represents Jesus Christ, our ultimate Bridegroom. How interesting that in each case the bride didn't feel worthy, but the bridegroom saw her as beautiful.

Isn't that just how we are when we come into the presence of God? Suddenly we see ourselves as we truly are—sinners who have been selfish, impure, and lacking in virtue. But He covers us with His righteousness; though our sins are as scarlet, we can be made white as snow. The beginning of true beauty is being forgiven by God—cleansed, pure, and made beautiful in His sight.

15. Ruth and Boaz

In the historical book of Ruth, Ruth was a Moabite—a people who worshiped the god Moab, who demanded child sacrifice and endorsed sexual immorality. By the sixteenth verse of Ruth 1, we see her putting her trust in the one true God. When she meets Boaz (her future bridegroom and our Christ figure), their conversation is full of symbolism that is relevant to you and me.

A. How does Boaz show Ruth mercy in Ruth 2:8–9? How can you see Jesus in Boaz?

B. Describe Ruth's response in Ruth 2:10. Can you identify? If so, how?

In Ruth 2:12, Boaz describes Ruth as having come "under [God's] wings." The picture of being covered by the Lord is repeated many times in Scripture. We are poor, naked, and filthy, but God washes and covers us with His garment. This picture is repeated again in Ruth when she goes to Boaz and asks him literally "to spread the corner of [his] garment over [her]" (Ruth 3:9). It is reminiscent of Isaiah 1:18, which assures us that though our sins are as scarlet they shall be as white as snow.

    C. How do you see this picture clearly stated in 1 John 1:9?

    D. How does Boaz describe Ruth's beauty in Ruth 3:11? Why does he describe her this way?

16. The Shulamite Maiden and King Solomon

In the poetic book often called the Song of Songs, the Shulamite maiden, a young peasant girl, is overwhelmed yet also ashamed when the king takes notice of her. Though this is a literal love story, it could not be called the Song of Songs (the very best) if it was only an earthly love story. Hidden within the Shulamite maiden are you and I, and hidden within Solomon is Jesus.

    A. Describe the Shulamite's words and feelings when Solomon first looks at her in Song of Solomon 1:6. Can you identify? If so, how?

    B. How does he see her, according to Song of Solomon 2:2? 4:7?

    C. How it is possible that there is "no flaw" in her?

When we are cleansed by the blood of Christ, it is just as if we never sinned. We have no flaw in His eyes. We are clothed in His robes of righteousness.

17. If you have put your trust in the blood of Jesus Christ, can you describe briefly how His forgiveness makes you feel?

Can you now repeat 1 John 1:5 without looking at it? Cover the following verse and recite it, looking only as necessary:

This is the message we have heard from him and declare to you: God is light; in him there is no darkness at all.

DAY 4
The Refining Process

Our forgiveness is the beginning of our beauty, but it is an ongoing process. That process can be painful. A third Old Testament love story can be found in the prophetic book of Hosea. In this story, God asks the prophet Hosea (who again is our Christ figure, his name meaning "God has saved") to marry an unfaithful woman.

Some are shocked, saying, "This couldn't have really happened, for God wouldn't have asked a prophet to marry an unfaithful woman." Bible teacher James Montgomery Boice, in *The Minor Prophets* (Baker Books, 1983, p. 17), writes:

If Hosea's story cannot be real … then neither is the story of salvation real, because that is precisely what Christ has done for us.

He has purchased us for himself to be a bride "without stain or wrinkle or any other blemish, but holy and blameless" (Eph. 5:27), and he has done this even though he knew in advance that we would often prove faithless.

God wants to paint a portrait for His unfaithful people. Hosea's wife, Gomer, runs after her lovers, and Hosea's heart is broken. Through this scene, God explains why He must discipline His unfaithful people. But Hosea looks forward to the day when his bride will return, be faithful, and have the inner beauty God so longs for in His people.

This is a challenging book, but there are a few key principles that, if grasped, may be helpful to you. Though Hosea is about the corporate bride, and specifically about Israel at that time, there are still applications for us today.

Like Israel, though we may know the Lord, each of us has a tendency toward unfaithfulness. We run after "other lovers," thinking God may not be quite enough—we overeat, yearn for the praise of man, or buy things we will never even use, thinking we need these things to be happy. God may need to take us into the wilderness to refine us, but His heart for us is always good, always desiring to help us become holy brides, "without stain or wrinkle or any other blemish."

18. Read Hosea 1—2.

    A. What does God ask Hosea to do and why?

    B. Describe the heart of the bride, according to Hosea 2:4–5.

    C. Describe some of the tough and tender ways God plans to bring His bride to her senses, according to Hosea 2:12–13.

    D. Hosea looks ahead to a different day when God's bride will be faithful. Describe his vision in Hosea 2:16 and also 2:19–20.

19. In what ways has God refined you? Has He ever taken you into the "wilderness" and spoken tenderly to you? If so, share something about it.

Can you say 1 John 1:5 by heart?

DAY 5

The King Will Greatly Desire Your Beauty

In the letters of John you will discover beauty secrets that will help you "be confident and unashamed before him at his coming" (1 John 2:28). We have a wonderful King who is returning for His bride one day, and in His absence, we should prepare for Him just as a bride prepares for her groom on her wedding day.

To close this week's lesson, Psalm 45 gives us a portrait of a glorious Bridegroom (Christ) and a bride who is being transformed to be like Him as she forsakes the world and devotes herself to Him.

In this study, you'll be encouraged to sing hymns and praise songs (see Hymns Index) to prepare your heart each day. Many of these songs are either verses from 1 John or songs that focus on the beauty of our King. Charles Spurgeon writes, "Jesus reveals himself when we are pouring forth our affections toward Him" (*The Treasury of David*, Vol. I,

Hendrickson, p. 316). This is what happened to the psalmist, and it can happen to us too. Today before you begin, sing "I Stand in Awe of You."

20. Read Psalm 45.

A. How do you sense the excitement of the psalmist as he begins to describe that great and wonderful day?

B. In verse 2, the phrase "fairer" (KJV) actually means "beautiful, beautiful" in Hebrew! He is beautiful beyond description." Find some of the descriptions of His beauty in verses 2–9.

C. What instructions are given to us in verses 10–11?

We often hear about how Jesus loves us, but we don't fully understand how He longs for our love, for a bride with undivided attention. "Forget[ting] [our] people and [our] father's house" (v. 10) is a metaphor for forsaking the world. Charles Spurgeon writes,

Wholehearted love is the duty and bliss of the marriage state in every case, but especially so in this lofty, mystic marriage. The church must forsake all others and cleave to Jesus only, or she will not please him nor enjoy the full manifestation of his love.... Jesus sees a beauty in his church, a beauty which he delights in most when it is not marred by worldliness. (Treasury of David, Vol. I, Hendrickson, p. 320)

D. How is the beauty of the bride described in verses 13–14?

21. What makes a woman truly beautiful? Summarize the important points from this week.

22. What do you think you will particularly remember? Why?

PRAYER TIME

Many are intimidated by the idea of praying out loud, but this guide will gently lead you into it and teach you some simple, yet very effective, ways to pray. One of the best ways is to pray using Scripture.

For example, if you were to pray using the following verses from Psalm 45 in groups of three, it might sound something like this:

(Psalm 45:1–2; Psalm 45:6; Psalm 45:10–11)

Amy reads Psalm 45:1–2:
My heart is stirred by a noble theme
as I recite my verses for the king;
my tongue is the pen of a skillful writer.

You are the most excellent of men
and your lips have been anointed with grace,
since God has blessed you forever.

Mary responds:
My heart is stirred by this theme.
I praise You, Jesus, for being so excellent.

Ellen reads:
Your throne, O God, will last
for ever and ever;
a scepter of justice will be
the scepter of your kingdom.

Amy responds:
Help me see things as You do, Lord—
with an eternal perspective.

Ellen responds:
And to remember that justice will prevail in the end.

Mary reads:
Listen, O daughter, consider and give ear:
Forget your people and your father's house.
The king is enthralled by your beauty;
honor him, for he is your lord.

Ellen responds:
May I listen, O Lord.

Mary responds:
May I listen, too.

Amy responds:
Help me forget the things that are not important
and concentrate on You.

Ellen says:
In Jesus name, Amen.

Now you try. Recite the same (or different) verses in groups of three and respond as you are led. God isn't looking for lofty prayers, but rather prayers from the heart.

Prayers & Praises

_____

_____

_____

_____

_____

_____

_____

_____

_____

_____

_____

Two

Beautiful Beyond Description
1 John 1:1–4

Have you ever thought, *I want to be the kind of beautiful woman God wants me to be, but I am so weak! I try but I fail!*

One of the first and most important beauty secrets has to do with beholding Jesus. As we look to Jesus, beholding more of His character, we trust Him and love Him more. As we do that, we become like Him. John Piper, in *The Pleasures of God* (Multnomah, 2000, p. 20), explains, "Beholding is a way of becoming," translating 2 Corinthians 3:18 as:

> *We all, with unveiled face, beholding the glory of the Lord,*
> *are being changed into his likeness from one degree of glory to another.*

"To see God," Piper says, "is to be changed by Him."

If you were raised in a Christian home, your parents helped you "behold" Jesus from a young age. If you were not raised in a Christian home, God still has His ways of causing you to wonder about Him. My first memory of an awareness of God occurred when I was about three years old. Alone in my father's library, whirling around and waving my hands dramatically to Beethoven's "Fifth," I suddenly had a profound thought, *Who made my hands?* Just as quickly, the answer came. God made your hands. God!

My first awareness of Jesus came through Christmas and its carols. On Christmas Eve at a candlelight service, we sang "O Holy Night" and I thought, *This really happened: the baby, the star, the shepherds ... Wow! Jesus!* When we sang the verse in "O Come All Ye Faithful" that says, "Word of the Father, now in flesh appearing ..." I was in awe, and though I only understood in part, it was the beginning of my transformation.

In the Hymns Index of this guide are hymns and praise choruses for you to begin each day in worship. Worship can open the heart for God's Spirit to slip truths in.

WARMUP

Think back to a time in your childhood or young adulthood when something caused you to wonder about God. What was it?

DAY 1

Jesus Is the Word

The author of the letters of John is also the author of the beloved gospel of John. He is John the apostle, the youngest disciple, who according to history outlived all the others.

John was with Jesus: he "beheld His glory" (John 1:14 NKJV), he laid his head on Jesus' breast, he ran to the empty tomb on Easter morning, and he was with the resurrected Christ when Jesus appeared and asked His disciples to touch Him, for "a ghost does not have flesh and bones, as you see I have" (Luke 24:39).

John was there at Pentecost when tongues of fire came down, and he played an integral part in the early church. But Christianity had been around for a while, and many became second or even third generation Christians. William Barclay writes:

In the first days of Christianity there was a glory and a splendour, but now Christianity has become a thing of habit, "traditional, half-hearted, nominal." Men had grown used to it and something of the wonder was lost…. John was writing at a time when, for some at least, the first thrill was gone and the flame of devotion had died to a flicker. (The Letters of John and Jude, Westminster Press, p. 3)

Both in his gospel and now again in his letters, John wants us to know—Jesus is God! We must behold Him as such for our lives to be transformed. Today we behold Him as the Word.

Prepare your heart in your time alone with God by singing the last verse and chorus of "O Come All Ye Faithful":

Yea, Lord, we greet Thee, born this happy morning; Jesus, to Thee be all glory given; Word of the Father, now in flesh appearing: O come let us adore Him, O come let us adore Him, O come let us adore Him, Christ the Lord.

Begin memorizing this week's verse, 1 John 1:6 (These verses are also in the Hymns Index if you want to tear out the page for your mirror, kitchen sink, etc.):

That which was from the beginning, which we have heard, which we have seen with our eyes, which we have looked at and our hands have touched—this we proclaim concerning the Word of life.

This week you will be making some comparisons between John's gospel and John's letters. His gospel is the fourth book in the New Testament; whereas, his letters are near the end of the New Testament.

1. What similarities do you find in the following three openings?

   A. Genesis 1:1

   B. John 1:1

   C. 1 John 1:1

2. Another similarity is John's distinctive name for Jesus, "the Word." How does John use it in John 1:1?

3. What else do you learn about the Word in John 1:3?

4. Turn back to Genesis. What repetition do you find in Genesis 1:3, 1:6, 1:9, 1:11, 1:14, 1:20, 1:24, and 1:26?

5. How do you think this might be related to Jesus being called "the Word"?

6. What other reasons can you think of for Jesus being called "the Word"? (One can be found in 1 John 2:14.)

7. When did Jesus begin?

> *Before the creation, the "Word" already existed. This is John's term for the preincarnate Christ.... John's theology consistently drives toward the conclusion that Jesus, the incarnate Word, is just as much God as God the Father.* (W. Hall Harris, *The Bible Knowledge Word Study*, Victor Books, 2002, p. 261)

8. When did you realize that Jesus did not begin at Christmas, but has always existed?

9. What does John tell us in John 1:14? When did this happen?

10. "The Word" can be both tender and terrifying. Certainly, as a baby in a manger, He is tender. The other book that John the apostle wrote is Revelation. Read Revelation 19:11–15 and describe "the Word" as He is presented here.

Here Jesus is coming back to wage war with the enemies of His bride. We see a parallel to Psalm 45 when the King comes in all His magnificence. We truly do have a Bridegroom coming on a white horse one day!

11. There is so much suffering in this world, both in the nations and in our individual lives. What do you particularly look forward to having Jesus one day bring an end to?

Begin memorizing 1 John 1:6:

> *If we claim to have fellowship with him yet walk in the darkness, we lie and do not live by the truth.*

DAY 2

Jesus Is the Great I AM

Another term for Jesus that permeates John's gospel is the great "I AM." Eight times in this distinctive gospel Jesus claims a different "I am." The great "I AM" is a clear allusion to Exodus 3:14 when Moses asked God to tell him His name. God replied, "I AM who I AM." God cannot say "I am like," because God is not like anyone or anything. Each time Jesus makes an "I am" proclamation in John's gospel, He is using the exact same words as God the Father spoke to Moses. Literally, it is *ego eimi,* or "I am" in two different ways. The Septuagint (the Greek translation of the Old Testament) shows us these are the same words. It is fascinating is to look at the responses of the people each time Jesus makes one of these pronouncements. His friends are in awe, but His enemies are angry.

Continue memorizing 1 John 1:6:

> *That which was from the beginning, which we have heard, which we have seen with our eyes, which we have looked at and our hands have touched—this we proclaim concerning the Word of life.*

12. Find the "I am" in each of the following passages, and then note any response you see from the people in the surrounding verses. Finally, comment on what this particular I AM means to you personally.

    A. John 6:35   I am _____

       Reaction?

       Means to you?

    B. John 8:12   I am _____

       Reaction?

       Means to you?

C. John 8:58 I am _____

   Reaction?

   Means to you?

D. John 10:7 I am _____

   Reaction?

   Means to you?

E. John 10:11 I am _____

   Reaction?

   Means to you?

F. John 11:25 I am _____

   Reaction?

   Means to you?

G. John 14:6 I am _____

   Reaction?

   Means to you?

H. John 15:1 I am _____

     Reaction?

     Means to you?

Jesus is the Eternal One who comes to this world. He comes as the Door, He comes as the Resurrection, He comes as the Light, He comes as the Way, and the Truth, and the Life, He comes as the Good Shepherd, He comes as the Vine, He is the One who before Abraham was, is. (R. C. Sproul, "Knowing Christ," Cassette 6, Ligonier Ministries, 1999)

13. If Jesus is, indeed, as much God as God the Father, what impact should that have on us?

When Kathy Troccoli and I were writing our study guide, *Forever in Love with Jesus*, one of the eight portraits of Christ we studied was the great "I am." I said to Kathy, "There's eight of them."

Kathy said, "Oh, He's been so many more than eight to me. When I lost my father, He said, 'I am your Father.' When financial responsibilities loomed ahead, He said, 'I am your Provider.' When I was caught in the chains of an eating disorder, He said, 'I am your Deliverer.' When the loneliness of being single hits me, He says, 'I am your Husband.'"

14. Name one way Jesus has been the great "I am" to you.

Continue memorizing 1 John 1:6:

If we claim to have fellowship with him yet walk in the darkness, we lie and do not live by the truth.

DAY 3

....

We Heard Him! We Saw Him! We Touched Him!

In some liturgical churches, the "Annunciation" is celebrated on the 25th of March. "Annunciation" means "to announce, to bring tidings." Gabriel announced to Mary that she would be "overshadowed by the Holy Spirit" to conceive Jesus. John 1 makes it clear this was not the beginning of Jesus' life, but simply the beginning of His time in the flesh. The Word made flesh, a paradox poets have pondered. John Donne calls it "immensity cloistered in a womb." Luci Shaw describes the enigma as "the Word, stern sentenced to be nine months dumb."

Read Luke 1:26–38.

Peter, James, and John were the three whom Jesus chose to take up the mountain to receive a glimpse of His future glory during the transfiguration. Jesus also chose these three to take to the Garden of Gethsemane where they caught a glimpse of His future suffering.

15. What are Peter and John trying to communicate in the following passages?

> *For we were not making up clever stories when we told you about the power of our Lord Jesus Christ and his coming again. We have seen his majestic splendor with our own eyes.* (2 Peter 1:16 NLT)

> *The Word became flesh and blood, and moved into the neighborhood. We saw the glory with our own eyes.* (John 1:14 MSG)

> *From the very first day, we were there, taking it all in—we heard it with our own ears, saw it with our own eyes, verified it with our own hands. The Word of Life appeared right before our eyes; we saw it happen!* (1 John 1:1–2 MSG)

16. Think of a time when you were acutely aware that Jesus was real, that He was, as Peter said, "no clever story," but that He really existed and truly cared about you.

17. John tells us in his gospel that "though the world was made through him, the world did not recognize him" (John 1:10). What evidence do you see that the world does not recognize Jesus, who existed from the beginning?

18. How do you imagine your life might be different if you did not know the One who is from the beginning?

19. Have you received new life and new power because of Jesus? If so, share how this manifested itself or when you were first aware of a difference in you because of Jesus.

Christianity is more than a religion, because every religion has one basic characteristic. Its followers are trying to reach God, find God, please God through their own efforts. Religions reach up toward God. Christianity is God reaching down to man. Christianity claims that men have not found God, but that God has found them. (Fritz Ridenour, How To Be A Christian without Being Religious, Regal Books, Introduction)

Can you now recite 1 John 1:5–6 without looking at it? Cover the following passage and recite it, looking only as necessary:

This is the message we have heard from him and declare to you: God is light; in him there is no darkness at all. If we claim to have fellowship with him yet walk in the darkness, we lie and do not live by the truth.

DAY 4
. . . .
So That You Also May Have Fellowship

It did not take long for divisions to spring up in the early church. False teachers arrived. Some people's first love of Jesus had faded. Others were wondering if He truly was God. John wrote emphatically to clarify: "Jesus is the Word, the eternal I am, the One who was from the beginning. They saw Him, they heard Him, they touched Him. This is not a fairy tale!"

When we realize who Jesus really is and are daily beholding Him, then will we have a fellowship unlike any other. There is excitement when we have fellowship with the living God and come together to share it. It is as if we are each bringing an ember from the fire of the living God, and igniting a bonfire that warms us all. Amy Carmichael writes:

How tepid is the love of so many who call themselves by His name. How tepid our own— my own—in comparison with the lava fires of His eternal love. I pray that you may be an ardent lover, the kind of lover who sets others on fire. (Candles in the Dark, Christian Literature Crusade, p. 107)

But in rich Christian fellowship, where hearts are aflame, friends will become more like Jesus. We are on a journey to meet our Bridegroom. John says, "Everyone who has this hope in Him purifies himself, just as He is pure" (1 John 3:3 NKJV). Part of the purification process occurs when believers who *truly* are having daily fellowship with Jesus come together and spur one another on.

20. Read 1 John 1:3–4 and follow the reasoning:

    A. Why, according to verse 3, is John proclaiming to us what he has seen and heard?

    B. With whom are John and the other disciples fellowshipping?

    C. What will be the end result according to verse 4?

The same word that John uses for fellowship is used in the opening of Philippians 2. Here again, Christians were experiencing division.

21. Read Philippians 2:1–11.

    A. What four appeals, beginning with the word "if," does Paul make in verse 1 for unity? After each example state how you have experienced this blessing of knowing Christ.

    "If" _____

    _____

    How have you experienced this? _____

    _____

    "If" _____

    _____

How have you experienced this? _____

"If"_____

_____

How have you experienced this? _____

_____

"If"_____

_____

How have you experienced this? _____

_____

B. What similarities do you see between Philippians 2:2 and 1 John 1:4? What is the significance of these similarities?

C. What things, according to Philippians 2:2, will make Paul's joy complete?

D. What further instructions in verses 3 and 4 will lead to rich Christian fellowship?

E. How does Paul emphasize the deity of Christ?

When we understand who Jesus is and embrace Him fully, when we experience being united with Him, when we are comforted by Him, when we realize that we have a greater compassion for our sisters and brothers because of Him, then we are headed toward the complete joy that both Paul and John write about.

22. The strength of Christian fellowship is dependent on the strength of each individual's fellowship with the Father and His Son, Jesus Christ. With that in mind, how can the individuals in this group help their fellowship be the best it can be?

Recite 1 John 1:5–6 by heart.

DAY 5

Your Joy Will Double Our Joy

Have you had the experience of helping someone discover the joy of the Lord? I remember how excited my neighbor Carol was upon encountering Jesus—she couldn't stop smiling, and her joy doubled my joy. Sometimes it isn't meeting Jesus for the first time, but encountering Him in a new way. One woman wrote:

> *I always knew Jesus loved me, but encountering Him as my Bridegroom through your studies has taken me to a whole new level. To think that He rejoices over me with singing. Everything has changed—I am not serving Him out of duty but out of sheer abandoned love!*

Seeing Carol's joy and having experienced it myself, bonded me not only with her, but with Christ.

Eugene Peterson paraphrases 1 John 1:3–4 (MSG):

> *We saw it, we heard it, and now we're telling you so you can experience it along with us, this experience of communion with the Father and his Son, Jesus Christ. Our motive for writing is simply this: We want you to enjoy this, too. Your joy will double our joy!*

Our motives for meeting together in Bible study should be similar. As we help one another walk in His light and His love, another wonderful thing will happen. The beauty of the Lord will grow in that individual, and she will come to study brimming with joy that will spread like a sweet fragrance to the whole group. This is the beauty of Christian fellowship. The word, "fellowship" (or "communion") as it is used here in the opening of John's letter, is a richly significant theological term. Stephen Smalley writes:

> *Christian fellowship is not the sentimental and superficial sharing of a random collection of individuals, but the profoundly mutual relationship of those who remain "in Christ," and therefore belong to each other.... The preposition "uera" (with us) emphasizes the deeply reciprocal relationship that can exist between one Christian and another.* (*Word Biblical Commentary,* V. 51, Word, 1984, p. 12)

23. Think of some times when Christian fellowship has been particularly sweet to you. Can you remember a small recent incident in this group? What else comes to mind?

24. How do you hope to see yourself and other members of this group encourage one another?

25. Summarize what you've learned in 1 John 1:1–4.

26. Write out 1 John 1:1 without looking at it.

27. What do you think you will remember from this lesson?

Recite 1 John 1:5–6 by heart.

PRAYER TIME

Another simple way to pray is in "conversational prayer," which some call "popcorn" prayer because short "pops" can come from anywhere. When the "popping" ceases, then it is another person's turn to share her need. In this prayer, we encourage you to share a need that is truly personal, rather than for a friend or relative. In becoming women of beauty, we need one another's prayer support. Lift up a way in which you long to become more like Jesus or a need that has been heavy on your heart. It also saves time to lift your need right in your prayer group rather than explaining it first. Break into groups of three or four.

31

Popcorn Prayer

1. An individual lifts a personal need to the Lord.

2. Others support her with short "pops" from anyone in the circle.

3. Continue until "popping" stops.

4. Another individual lifts a personal need to the Lord.

Three

A Woman of Beauty Walks in the Light

1 John 1:5–9

John wrote his gospel to help people believe that Jesus was the Christ, and in believing, that they have life through His name. His purpose for writing his letters was different.

In his letters, he writes to help believers increase their confidence that they really have that life and learn how to make that life complete. The prevailing message of 1 John is that:

Since God is light,
His child should walk in the light.

Since God is love,
His child should love.

Since God is compassion,
His child should show mercy.

Since God is truth,
His child should speak the truth.

J. B. Phillips puts it like this:

> *The life of a man who professes to be living in God must bear the stamp of Christ.*
> (1 John 2:6 PH)

If God is your Father, if Christ is your Brother, then you will look something like them. But there is another exciting truth that you must not miss, for it is the secret to becoming a woman of beauty. John Stott puts it like this:

> *Our love and our hatred not only reveal if we are in the light or the darkness, but actually contribute to the light or darkness in which we already are.* (*The Letters of John*, Eerdmans, 2000, p. 99)

WARMUP

Think of a recent time when you sensed God was speaking to you—either through His Word, His Spirit, or another believer. What was He saying and how did you respond?

DAY 1
. . . .

Real Beauty versus Counterfeit Beauty

The White Witch in the Narnia series has a "cool" exterior beauty, but underneath she has the characteristics of a child of Satan. She hates, lies, plans evil, and carries it out. Yet at first sight she looks quite enticing. Edmund is coaxed into her carriage, snuggles beneath her soft fur coat, and eats her Turkish delight.

One theme in 1 John is "real versus counterfeit." John gives us some characteristics to consider in discerning between the two. At first, when you read some of the tests, you may feel panic. The behavioral characteristics John describes sound very black and white.

1. Find some of John's "black-and-white" behavioral statements in the following passages:

A. 1 John 1:6

B. 1 John 2:4

C. 1 John 2:9

D. 1 John 2:15

E. 1 John 2:29

F. 1 John 3:6

G. 1 John 3:7

H. 1 John 3:8

I. 1 John 3:10

J. 1 John 3:17

K. 1 John 3:24

L. 1 John 4:7–8

M. 1 John 4:20

N. 1 John 5:3

O. 1 John 5:18

2. Is John saying that a true child of God never sins, always loves his brother, and always obeys? What does 1 John 1:8 say?

Since John clearly states that a child of God sins, how are we to understand his black-and-white statements? Another theme of 1 John is that we must become like the One who gave us birth. If our father is Satan, then we will become more and more like him as we mature, but if our Father is God, then we will become more and more like Him as we mature. We will either become a woman of light, love, and beauty, or a woman of darkness, hate, and deception.

Begin memorizing 1 John 1:7:

> *But if we walk in the light, as he is in the light, we have fellowship with one another, and the blood of Jesus, his Son, purifies us from all sin.*

DAY 2

Looking Like Our Father

John's gospel makes it clear that when we are "born again" a new life comes to live in us—the very life of God, born in us by His Spirit. This nature cannot sin; thus, the black-and-white statements of 1 John. J. B. Phillips paraphrases it like this:

> *The man who is really God's son does not practice sin, for God's nature is in him, for good, and such a heredity is incapable of sin.* (1 John 3:9)

3. Make a list of qualities that a child of God would have in contrast with a child of Satan.

Child of God	Child of Satan
1:7 _____	1:6 _____
2:3 _____	2:4 _____
2:10 _____	2:9 _____
2:17 _____	2:15 _____
3:9 _____	3:8 _____
3:16 _____	3:17 _____
4:7–8 _____	3:10 _____
4:2 _____	4:3 _____

Again, this list might be frightening, for every one of us has "shut up our compassions" to a brother in need, chosen sin, or failed in thought, word, and deed more often than we like to admit. Remember what John Stott said:

> *Our love and our hatred not only reveal if we are in the light or the darkness, but actually contribute to the light or darkness in which we already are.* (*The Letters of John*, Eerdmans, 2000, p. 99)

God's seed lives in us if we are born again, and that seed grows and flourishes as we mature. Another theme in 1 John is that as we choose to walk in the light, as we choose to love, as we choose to be compassionate, and as we choose to tell the truth, His life is made complete in us.

4. Read through the five short chapters of 1 John, looking for the word *complete*. Write down the verses you find.

Keep memorizing 1 John 1:7:

> *But if we walk in the light, as he is in the light, we have fellowship with one another, and the blood of Jesus, his Son, purifies us from all sin.*

DAY 3

God Is Light and in Him Is No Darkness at All

While on a ski vacation as a little girl, I attended an Easter Sunrise Service on top of a mountain in Aspen, Colorado. At 5:45 a.m., snow crunched under our boots as my family headed in the darkness to board the chairlift. As we ascended, we gazed in wonder at the stars above us. We pulled our blankets tightly around us for protection from the strong wind that whistled through the pines straight to our bones.

At the top we joined a growing crowd seated at picnic tables facing east. The panoramic sky grew lighter as we waited in hushed anticipation. Suddenly the bright red rim of the sun peeked from behind a lower mountain range. Slowly, surely, it flooded the sky with radiant splendor and our bodies with welcome warmth. Some enthusiastic young men with guitars led us in "Christ the Lord Is Risen Today!" and "Up from the Grave He Arose!" In the glory of that service, our cold chairlift ride was forgotten. Thinking back to that time today, I am reminded of Isaiah's prophecy:

The people walking in darkness have seen a great light; on those living in the land of the shadow of death a light has dawned (Isa. 9:2).

Read 1 John 1:5–7.

5. What do we learn about God in verse 5? What are some of the characteristics of light?

Betsie ten Boom, who died in a Nazi concentration camp, urged her sister Corrie to get the message out: "We must tell people what we have learned ... that no darkness can keep out God's marvelous light. They will believe us, because we've been there." (Joan Brown, *Corrie: The Lives She's Touched,* Revell, p. 72)

6. Throughout Scripture, God is associated with light. In each of the following, explain why you think the metaphor of light is used.

   A. "The LORD is my light and my salvation—whom shall I fear? The LORD is the strong-hold of my life—of whom shall I be afraid?" (Ps. 27:1).

   B. "Praise be to the name of God for ever and ever; wisdom and power are his ... He reveals deep and hidden things; he knows what lies in darkness, and light dwells with him" (Dan. 2:20, 22).

   C. "When Jesus spoke again to the people, he said, 'I am the light of the world. Whoever follows me will never walk in darkness, but will have the light of life'" (John 8:12).

Can you recite 1 John 1:5-7 without looking at it? Recite the following passage, looking only as necessary:

This is the message we have heard from him and declare to you: God is light; in him there is no darkness at all. If we claim to have fellowship with him yet walk in the darkness, we lie and do not live by the truth. But if we walk in the light, as he is in the light, we have fellowship with one another, and the blood of Jesus, his Son, purifies us from all sin.

7. How does the truth of 1 John 1:5 lead to the conclusion of verse 6?

God simply cannot follow you into darkness, for in Him there is no darkness.

8. Share a time when you were aware you were losing fellowship with God because you
   had wandered into darkness.

If you get out of the light, you become a sentimental Christian, and live only on your memories, and your testimony will have a hard metallic ring to it. Beware of trying to cover up your present refusal to "walk in the light" by recalling your past experiences when you did "walk in the light." (Oswald Chambers, *My Utmost for His Highest*, Discovery House, pp. 8, 13)

Read and memorize 1 John 1:7 in the *Amplified Bible*:

But if we [really] are living and walking in the Light, as He [Himself] is in the Light, we have [true, unbroken] fellowship with one another, and the blood of Jesus Christ His Son cleanses (removes) us from all sin and guilt [keeps us cleansed from sin in all its forms and manifestations].

9. Meditate on the above verse.

   A. What does it mean to "walk in the light as He is in the light?" Is this the same or
      slightly different than asking, "What would Jesus do?"

   B. We've already seen that living in the light gives us fellowship with God, who must
      stay in the light. Now, what other blessing is promised in the first part of
      1 John 1:7?

   C. Why is it that when we walk out of the light it hurts our relationships with one
      another? Give examples.

   D. What second blessing is promised in the second part of verse 7? What does this
      imply?

Because of our deceptive hearts, there is so much sin we cannot even see. All we can do is ask God's Spirit to search us and repent of what we can see—and He will graciously cover the rest.

    E. What does "living in the light" look like? (You may need to look ahead to 1 John 1:8–9.)

    F. Can you see how living in the light would bring richness to your fellowship with other believers? Give examples.

PRIVATE ACTION ASSIGNMENT

If there is a wall between you and another believer, have you brought everything to light? Have you confessed and sincerely repented of any darkness on your part? If not, please do so. If you need to go to her to confess and ask forgiveness, do. Don't tell her what she did wrong, but confess any darkness on your part. Repentance if a gift from God, so ask for it (2 Tim. 2:25).

DAY 4

A Child of God Responds to the Light

When our daughter Sally was eighteen, she went to a youth conference where she was told, "When God speaks to you and you shut Him out, a callous forms on your heart, and the next time, it's harder to hear Him." The following summer Sally went to see Forrest Gump with her brother and his girlfriend. Sally tells the story:

> *I was eating popcorn and thoroughly enjoying this really cute movie. But about halfway through, suddenly a scene came where one of the characters was saying terrible things about Jesus. I became very uncomfortable. I thought, I hope this scene passes quickly, so I can enjoy the movie again. And then I heard it. It wasn't an audible voice, but it was an impression on my heart that was so strong that I knew it was from the Lord. Only two words. Just go.*

> *My first reaction was No way! I spent good money, and I'm enjoying this. I haven't been to a movie in forever! But then I heard it again. Just go.*

> *I thought, OK, Lord. I leaned over to my brother and his girlfriend and I said, "J. R., let's just go."*

> *J. R. and his girlfriend looked at each other, and I could tell they were going through exactly the same struggle I had just been through—the struggle to obey God's voice. They both hesitated and then looked thoughtfully at the screen.*

More blasphemy! Suddenly they agreed, "OK! Let's go!" The three of us got up and walked out of the theatre, and it felt so good to know we had heard and obeyed!

If you want to have fellowship with God, stay in the light. The moment we consciously ignore His quiet voice and walk into the darkness, we cut off our fellowship (not our relationship) with Him. To resume fellowship, you must confess your sin and return to the light. If you refuse, you will walk further and further into the darkness, until the darkness blinds you.

What Sally was taught is true: "A callous forms on your heart." The difference between humans and animals is that we have a conscience, but if we keep ignoring that still, small voice, we can become like brute beasts. Romans 1 states that the people ignored God, so their "foolish hearts were darkened"; then they continued down their dark path, and God "gave them up to the lusts of their hearts." Soon they were in bondage, not only practicing improperly, but teaching others to do the same.

10. Read John 8:2–12.

    A. What challenge did Jesus make to the Pharisees who brought the woman caught in adultery? What did the Spirit reveal to each of them?

    B. What should the above teach us?

    C. What two things did Jesus tell the woman in verse 11?

    D. What application might there be for you in the above verse?

    E. What two-fold promise for the one who follows Jesus is in John 8:12?

Not only will we not walk in darkness, but we will also have the light of life. Psalm 25:14 says, "The Lord confides in those who fear him; he makes his covenant known to them." We become wiser, more sensitive to His promptings, and farther and farther away from brute beasts.

11. Read John 8:31–35.

   A. What promise is in verse 32?

   B. How did the Pharisees argue with this?

   C. How did Jesus respond?

12. Read John 8:36–47.

   A. What argument ensues?

   B. What evidence does Jesus give that their father is Satan rather than God?

   C. How do you see this paralleling the teaching in 1 John?

13. Read John 8:48–59 and outline the argument in this passage.

14. Summarize what you have learned today and how you might apply it to your life.

Can you recite 1 John 1:5–7 by heart?

DAY 5

. . . .

A Woman of Beauty Keeps Her Clothes Clean

We're going to get dirty—the narrow path is like a log running across a mucky swamp. We will slip. But how long we stay in the muck reveals to whom we belong.

Reluctance to admit wrongdoing affects our relationship with God and others. Once, when speaking at a conference about the sins that hurt our friendships, I mentioned laziness. A young woman came up to me afterward and told me the following story:

> *Two years ago my closest friend moved away for a year. We promised to write during that year apart. However, I didn't. The reason I gave her when she moved back was that I'd had a baby and had been so busy. However, when I tried to resume our friendship, I ran into a wall!*
>
> *Tonight, when you talked about the sin of laziness, the Holy Spirit convicted me. My friend was here, so right afterward I went over to her and said: "The reason I didn't write wasn't because I was too busy, but because I was too lazy! I didn't see that until tonight. I was wrong and I'm so sorry I hurt you. I miss you so much. Will you forgive me?" We both started to cry and flung our arms around each other. The wall came tumbling down!*

Just as confession can restore fellowship with a friend, so can it restore fellowship with God. The moment we realize we've walked into the dark, we must confess our sins. No excuses. No partial turns. We must turn completely and walk in the other direction.

15. Meditate on 1 John 1:9–10. What promise is in verse 9?

16. There is also both a true and a counterfeit repentance. Think of a sin with which you struggle. Give some examples of "counterfeit repentance." Then describe what "true repentance" looks like.

17. When we attempt to cover our sins or justify them, what two warnings are given in verse 10?

Pray through 1 John 1:5–9 in the *New Living Translation* in your personal quiet time. First read the verse, next the suggestion for prayer in bold, and then write or say your prayer aloud.

This is the message he has given us to announce to you: God is light and there is no darkness in him at all.

Praise God for His purity and holiness. Sing a hymn or song about His holiness, and mean it with your whole heart.

So we are lying if we say we have fellowship with God but go on living in spiritual darkness. We are not living in the truth.

Ask God, and be still before Him—how is it between us? Write down anything He shows you and turn from any sin.

But if we are living in the light of God's presence, just as Christ is, then we have fellowship with each other, and the blood of Jesus, his Son, cleanses us from every sin.

Ask God, how is it between me and my brothers and sisters? Be still before Him and attentive to His voice. Write down anything He shows you.

If we say we have no sin, we are only fooling ourselves and refusing to accept the truth.

Accept His truth about yourself, and turn from any sin He has shown you.

But if we confess our sins to him, he is faithful and just to forgive us and to cleanse us from every wrong.

Trust His forgiveness and cleansing power, and thank Him for it.

18. What do you think you will particularly remember from this week's lesson?

Prayers & Praises

_____

_____

_____

_____

_____

_____

_____

_____

_____

_____

_____

_____

_____

Four

A Woman of Beauty Walks in Love
1 John 2:1–17

First John is a like an orchestral piece. The theme reflects the beauty of our King, but that beauty is manifested in three ways: light, love, and truth. This theme of beauty is introduced with gentle string instruments representing light, then wind instruments join in with the sound of love, and soon the percussion instruments beat the importance of truth. All manifestations continue, sometimes more prominent than another, all building to a full orchestral triumph.

In the second chapter, the theme of love is added, but light is still playing. The children's chorus in the Hymns Index, "Beloved, Let Us Love One Another," will be an easy way for you to memorize this new theme. It is based on the *King James Version*, so memorize 1 John 4:7–8 in this version.

> *Beloved, let us love one another: for love is of God; and every one that loveth is born of God, and knoweth God. He that loveth not knoweth not God; for God is love.*

WARMUP
Name one thing which has given you fleeting happiness and then explain why that happiness didn't last.

DAY I

A Woman of Beauty Continues in the Light

Before the wind instruments join in with their theme of love, the strings continue alone for the opening of chapter 2. The theme of walking in the light is reiterated, but also clarified, as we are told that one who walks in the light is one who keeps His commandments.

Review 1 John 1:5–7.

Prepare your heart through worship—either with songs from the Hymns Index or by using your hymnal. Meditate on the words and give God the sacrifice of praise.

1. Meditate on 1 John 2:1–2.

    A. According to 1 John 2:1, why does John write?

    B. Choose an area of sin, such as lying or sexual immorality, and explain why it is always better not to sin in the first place than to repent of that sin.

    C. What are some areas in which you struggle, but that you know if you do not sin, you will be spared grief?

    D. If we do sin, however, who do we have according to the second part of 1 John 2:1? What does this mean?

    E. Propitiation (1 John 2:2 KJV) is a sacrifice that is meant to take away the enmity brought by sin between God and the worshiper. Why is Christ the only One who can be a propitiation for us?

2. What truth from chapter 1 is reiterated in 2:3–4? Do you find any further clarification in these verses?

3. What two promises can you find in 1 John 2:5?

4. What truth from chapter 1 is reiterated in 2:6?

DAY 2

The Most Important Things Are Said When Time Is Running Out

Now the wind instruments join in, introducing the theme of love. John seems to speak in riddles, saying this is not new, and yet it is! What does he mean?

The commandment to love is as old as Leviticus, where we are told to love our neighbor as ourselves (Lev. 19:18). Yet John, both in his gospel and again in this letter, talks about a "new command." The first time we heard about this "new" command was at the last supper when Jesus was washing the feet of His disciples.

One of the things that I see, both in Scripture and in life, is that important things are said as time is running out. When my fifty-nine-year-old husband realized that cancer was going to take his life, he called each of his children, one by one, to his bed. Our youngest curled up next to him as he wept and told her he was so sorry he had to leave her, but that he was so glad he got to be her daddy. He told her how much he loved her. She will never forget his words; the most important things are said when time is running out.

Time was running out on earth for Jesus as well, and He knew it.

At the last supper, and again in His last recorded prayer before the cross, He said the same thing, and it has to do with this new commandment that runs throughout the first letter of John. Today we will consider this context from John's gospel before we return to the letter.

5. Describe the setting in John 13:1. Note the time, what Jesus knew, and how He was feeling.

6. What happened in John 13:21–30?

7. How does Jesus address the remaining eleven in John 13:33?

John uses the address "little children" seven times in his letter. Just as Jesus used this endearing term, now the aged apostle uses it for us.

8. Meditate on the new commandment in John 13:34.

   A. What is it? Write down everything you find.

   B. How is it different from loving our neighbor?

9. How will people know that we are His disciples, according to John 13:35?

Francis Schaeffer points out that Jesus says that non-Christians will recognize us if we have love.

> *The point is, it is possible to be a Christian without showing the mark, but if we expect non-Christians to know that we are Christians, we must show the mark.* (*The Mark of a Christian*, Intervarsity Press, p. 133)

10. Can you remember a time, either as a non-Christian or as a new Christian, when you were struck by love between a group of believers? Share what you remember and why you remember it.

11. Read John 17:20–23.

   A. For whom is Jesus praying here?

   B. In verse 21, what exactly does He pray, and what does He say will be the result?

   C. How does He elaborate on this in verse 23?

D. How is this "last" prayer similar to the words Jesus spoke to His disciples at the Last Supper?

12. As you look at your own life, how well do you love:

A. The believers in your local church?

B. True believers in denominations that embrace Christ but are quite different on peripheral issues from your own denomination?

C. Believers who may have little to give you personally in return for your love—perhaps they are poor, elderly, or in faraway mission fields?

D. Believers who, for a myriad of reasons, may be slightly "irregular"?

Memorize 1 John 4:7–8:

Beloved, let us love one another: for love is of God; and every one that loveth is born of God, and knoweth God. He that loveth not knoweth not God; for God is love.

DAY 3

A Woman of Beauty Grows in Radiance as She Loves

When we adopted Annie, a five-year-old from an orphanage in Seoul, she was withdrawn and unresponsive. Yet God provided a six-year-old friend for Annie who reflected God's marvelous light and love. I'll never forget the day they met. Sarena placed a teddy bear in Annie's arms. Annie threw the teddy bear to the ground.

Sarena reached out for Annie's hand. Annie jerked her hand away. Sarena said, "Annie, I just want to be your friend!" Annie didn't understand English, and she just scowled at Sarena.

I fully expected Sarena to give up. The most natural response to pain and rejection is withdrawal. But Sarena didn't respond naturally, she responded supernaturally. She turned to me and said, "I don't care how long it takes, Mrs. Brestin. I am just going to keep on being nice to Annie, and one day we are going to be best friends."

In time, God's marvelous light shined through Sarena and thawed the frozen heart of our little Annie. Though only six, Sarena was beautiful in Christ. Today Sarena is a young woman who is radiant in His love.

13. Can you explain the riddle of 1 John 2:7–8?

14. Contrast everything you can find in verses 9–11 between:

The brother who loves   The "brother" who hates

15. Remember John Stott's statement that "our love or our hate not only reveal if we are in the light or the darkness, but actually contribute to the light or the darkness in which we already are." How is his statement supported by verses 9–11?

16. An enormous factor is being a true woman of beauty is increasing light, purity, and radiance. How does Psalm 34:5 picture this?

17. How can you see the above truth illustrated in the individuals in the following verses?

A. Acts 7:9–10

B. Acts 7:54–60

C. Ruth 2:11; 3:11

Can you say 1 John 4:7–8 by heart?

DAY 4

A Woman of Beauty is Winsome

It's a challenge to be winsome yet not worldly.

A woman should look like a woman and enjoy her feminine charms. We aren't going to be winsome representatives of the gospel if we are dreary, prim, slovenly, or immodest. We should care about how we look. But it is so easy to become conformed to the world and be more concerned with our hair than our hearts, to put more thought on what goes into our mouths than what goes into our minds, and to spend more money on makeup than on mercy.

Likewise, a home should be a haven, and we should use the creative gifts God has given us to make it a place of beauty and order. A winsome woman knows how to create ambience to bless her family and all kinds of people in a cold and hurting world. Also, if our home is neglected it can become a disgrace to the gospel (Tit. 2:5). But again, it is so easy to get out of balance, caring more about the interior decoration than about the interior kindness, wisdom, and joy, or to think more about impressing the neighbors than pleasing God.

Today we'll take a side route into scriptural passages to consider the importance of winsomeness; tomorrow we'll return to 1 John to consider how to be alert to ways the enemy tries to throw us off balance, turning winsomeness into worldliness.

Proverbs 31 sings of a woman's practical abilities, and the Song of Solomon sings of a woman's charm and beauty. Both of these passages can seem overwhelming to us, for the standards are amazingly high. How many of us can do all the Proverbs 31 woman does—from dabbling in real estate to weaving luxurious garments of purple? How many of us can compare to the Shulammite maiden, who had a neck like a *Vogue* model and breasts like a sexual goddess?

It may comfort you to know that both Proverbs 31 and the Song of Solomon, on a symbolic level, picture the bride of Christ. The beauty of the bride in the Song of Solomon represents the perfect beauty of a bride in love and abandoned to her husband. When we love Christ like that, when we are abandoned to Him, we are so beautiful to Him, giving Him the same joy as the lovely Shulammite maiden gave Solomon. The beauty of the bride in Proverbs 31 is a composite bride, for it would take *many* to do all she does. Yet both of these passages can help us realize that our feminine gifts are indeed gifts, and if kept in balance can delight and bless.

18. In the following passages, how do you see the bride in the Song of Solomon yearning for and delighting in her bridegroom?

A. Song of Solomon 1:2

B. Song of Solomon 2:3–4

C. Song of Solomon 2:16

19. What evidence do you see in your life that you yearn for more of Christ and delight in Him?

When we are in love with Jesus, we have the same radiance as a bride who is in love, and others are drawn, not only to us, but also to Him!

20. Describe the beauty Solomon sees in his bride. Consider as well what the symbolic level might be, for God is looking for a pure, faithful, and abandoned bride.

A. Song of Solomon 4:6–7

This is the second time Solomon has asked his bride to come higher with him. The first time (2:14), she was camped out in the clefts of the rock, the hiding places, and would not show him her face. We can become complacent in our Christian walk and refuse to obey. Though God will not force us, how delighted He is when we come willingly, going to the "mountain of myrrh" (myrrh is symbolic of death), dying to ourselves and living to Him. This makes her beautiful to Him.

B. Song of Solomon 4:12

A "garden locked up" symbolizes a virgin, and God is looking for a pure "virgin" who has not run after other gods. This makes her beautiful to Him.

21. What evidence do you see in your life that you desire purity and that you are willing to die to yourself and to live to Christ?

22. On an implied level, what evidence can you find in The Song of Solomon that we should care about our physical appearance?

In Proverbs 31, Lemuel's mother guides him on what to look for in an ideal wife. Again, on a symbolic level, this is the bride of Christ. But here we see more of her practical side than her physical or feminine charm.

23. In Proverbs 31:10, what quality does Lemuel's mother mention first, and how highly is it valued?

24. What do you learn about her relationship to her husband in Proverbs 31:11-12?

25. What various character qualities does each of the following descriptions exemplify?
   A. Proverbs 31:13-17

   B. Proverbs 31:18

"Her lamp does not go out at night" doesn't mean she works late into the night (for He gives His beloved sleep, according to Psalm 127:2), but that she has remembered to have a supply of oil on hand. She is an organized woman (who checks off a list at the grocery store) so she isn't caught by surprise.

   C. Proverbs 31:20

   D. Proverbs 31:21–22

The clothing for herself, her family, and her home (bedding and upholstery) is not cheap, but classy! She uses fine material and is an excellent seamstress. There is at least the implication here that God is supportive of our using our gifts to make ourselves and our homes appealing.

   E. Proverbs 31:25

F. Proverbs 31:27

G. Proverbs 31:28–29

26. What is the balanced perspective of charm and physical beauty, according to Proverbs 31:30?

DAY 5

A Woman of Beauty is not Worldly

We have an enemy who wants to pervert whatever is good. It is good to care about our appearance, but if we think that is what matters most, we are in trouble. It is good to want to make our home a haven, but if it becomes our identity and we lust for bigger and better, then we are off balance. Our enemy continually whispers lies to pervert good gifts from God. For example, sex within marriage is God's good gift, but the enemy uses the lust of the flesh to lure individuals outside of the healthy boundaries of marriage. Food is God's good gift as well, but it becomes harmful when lust turns it to gluttony. Work is a good gift from God, but when pride turns it into our identity and craving for more applause from men, the enemy has been successful in perverting it.

The enemy has also taken a woman's desire to be physically lovely and to have a beautiful home and perverted it by telling her the lie that what matters most is the physical. This is who you are, he lies, so give your life to it.

27. First, John addresses believers in various levels of spiritual maturity in 1 John 2:12–14, reminding them of their particular strength in Christ. Write down what he says to each of the following people and then explain why this might be helpful in overcoming the influence of the world.

A. Young believers (little children)

B. More mature believers (young men)

C. The most mature believers (fathers)

Read 1 John 2:15–17 in the *English Standard* version translation.

Do not love the world or the things in the world. If anyone loves the world, the love of the Father is not in him. For all that is in the world—the desires of the flesh and the desires of the eyes and pride in possessions—is not from the Father but is from the world. And the world is passing away along with its desires, but whoever does the will of God abides forever.

28. What command and corresponding reason does John give in 1 John 2:15?

Now read the same passage in the J. B. Phillips paraphrase:

Never give your hearts to the world or to any of the things in it. A man cannot love the Father and love the world at the same time. For the whole world-system, based as it is on men's primitive desires, their greedy ambitions and the glamour of all that they think splendid, is not derived from the Father at all, but from the world itself. The world and all its passionate desires will one day disappear. But the man who is following God's will is part of the permanent and cannot die.

29. Name the three categories of temptation. What does each mean? Give an example of each.

30. What reason is given, in verse 17, for not "giving your heart" to the world?

31. It is a good to desire to make your home a haven, a place of order and ambience so that it might bring joy and comfort to others. Now, considering 1 John 2:15–17, how might the enemy take this good desire and pervert it?

32. Likewise, it is good to desire to be physically appealing, a winsome representative of Christ, and a blessing to one's husband and loved ones. How might the enemy take this good desire and pervert it?

33. What truths do you need to keep speaking into your soul so that you can be protected from the lies of the enemy in regard to physical beauty both in your person and your home?

34. What do you expect to remember from this lesson?

PRAYER TIME

Cluster in groups of two or three, and pray for your character through the following Scripture passages: 1 John 1:5–7, 1 John 2:15–17, and 1 John 4:7–8.

Prayers & Praises

_____

_____

_____

_____

_____

_____

_____

_____

_____

_____

_____

_____

_____

Five

A Woman of Beauty Walks in Truth
1 John 2:18–29

John's symphonic piece continues, growing more complex, more beautiful. The string instruments continue with light, the wind instruments continue with love, and now the percussion instruments enter, beating out the importance of truth.

A woman of beauty is not an airhead. She has a discerning mind and recognizes the signs of the enemy. She is very alert to the central lie of the enemy but also can spot the smaller red flags. She knows she needs to be immersed in God's truth so that she can be an overcomer.

Corrie ten Boom was an overcomer. Though Hitler claimed to be a believer, she knew he failed all the tests. Though many believers at this time failed to walk in the truth, instead desiring to preserve their own lives, the truth of God so permeated the souls of the ten Boom family that they risked their physical lives to hide the Jews. They were caught, but continued to be overcomers.

One night Corrie climbed out of her barracks when she heard that 250 prisoners were being taken to an unknown destination, perhaps, to their death. In a place hidden from the guards, she found ways to encourage her brothers and sisters with the truth. She tells the story:

"Jesus is Victor!" I whispered.

"Oh, Corrie—how could you? Go back to your barracks!"

"Fear not. Only believe."

"Thank you, Corrie. God bless you."

"Underneath are the everlasting arms. Jesus has said, 'I am with you till the end of the world.' Look to the Lord. He loves you. Jesus is Victor!"

Corrie said, "There was joy in my heart as the Holy Spirit gave me a short message for everyone that went through the gate." (Joan Brown, *Corrie: The Lives She's Touched*, Revell, pp. 60–61)

WARMUP

We defeat the lies of the enemy with the Sword of the Spirit, which is the Word of God. Name a lie from the world or your own heart, and then name the truth from God's Word to speak to it.

DAY 1

· ·

She Holds to the Original Teaching

In John's day, there were those who were infiltrating and offering a "new and improved" Christianity. The same is true today. They tell us that there is a new way, a better way, a way that redefines the Scriptures and the identity of Jesus.

John warns us to hold to the original teaching and continually check the things that we hear and read with the Word of God, to see if they are true. It is clear that there are false teachers right within our churches, for false teachers begin in the church and then leave. But there is a period when they are still right within us, and we need to know the red flags so that we can spot them.

1. Read 1 John 2:18–21.

   A. What time does John say it is?

   B. Who does he say is coming? And who will precede him?

C. Then, as now, deniers of the Son called themselves Christians. What evidence does John give to show that they were never really part of the body of Christ?

D. What do true believers have, according to verse 20, to protect them?

E. What does John remind them of in verse 21?

F. Why is it important to continually remind ourselves of the basic truths of Christianity?

2. The central truths of Christianity have to do with the identity of Jesus and why He came. Who is Jesus and why did He come? Support your answers scripturally.

Begin memorizing 1 John 2:22. This is the ultimate test, the one that all antichrists fail.

Who is the liar? It is the man who denies that Jesus is the Christ. Such a man is the antichrist—he denies the Father and the Son.

DAY 2

She Recognizes the Red Flags

John continues stressing sticking to the original teaching. He gives some red flags to recognize the counterfeit. The first is the biggest.

3. What is the ultimate lie according to verse 22?

The words *Jesus* and *Christ* here are crucial. Kenneth Wuest explains that Jesus means "Jehovah saves" and contains the doctrine of the substitutionary atonement offered on the cross. Christ means "the anointed one: the Messiah."

The denial therefore is that the person called Jesus was neither God nor man, and that on the Cross He did not offer an atonement for sin. Present day Modernism denies the deity of Jesus of Nazareth and the substitutionary atonement He offered on the cross, while subscribing to His humanity. (Kenneth Wuest, *Word Studies in the New Testament*, Eerdmans, pp. 134–35)

4. The lie in 1 John 2:22 is central, but John gives several other clues to help us discern false teachers. Find the warning sign in each of the following verses:

A. 1 John 2:4

B. 1 John 2:9

C. 1 John 2:15

D. 1 John 2:19

E. 1 John 2:22

F. 1 John 2:23

G. 1 John 3:10

Many people call themselves Christians but have redefined Christianity in their own terms. They deny the deity of Christ and His sacrificial atonement. These are people who seemed to be believers in the beginning but then strayed from the original teaching.

DAY 3

She Will Keep Herself a Pure Virgin

When recording artist Kathy Troccoli and I did a video Bible study on "Falling in Love with Jesus," looking at Christ as our Bridegroom, there were those who were offended, saying that sexual images were inappropriate for Christian material. However, what they didn't realize was that their argument was not with us, but with the prophets of the Old Testament. Sexual images run throughout the Bible to picture the purity and the faithfulness of the "bride" God desires. Derek Kidner writes:

> *It is a bold and creative stroke by which God, instead of banning sexual imagery from religion, rescues and raises it to portray the ardent love and fidelity which are the essence of His covenant.* (*The Message of Hosea*, Intervarsity Press, 1981, p. 33)

In our opening lesson we looked at Psalm 45 and the picture of the royal Bridegroom coming for His bride. Jesus longs for us to be a radiant bride who has clung to the truth and therefore has been strengthened to keep herself pure. God uses the picture of a "pure virgin" as one who has not run after false gods and false teaching, but instead, has remained faithful to Him.

5. Find the sexual imagery in the following passages and then explain what God is trying to help us understand through it:

   A. Jeremiah 2:20

   B. Jeremiah 3:6–7

   C. Hosea 2:4–5

   D. Hosea 2:13

   E. 2 Corinthians 11:1–3

6. John reviews the themes of keeping ourselves pure for Christ in 1 John 2:24–29:

    A. What is the central warning? (v. 24)

    B. What promise is given to those who hold to the original teaching? (v. 25)

    C. Why must John write these things? (v. 26)

    D. Why it is possible for us to study the Bible on our own, and why is it important we do so? (v. 27)

John is not speaking against having teachers here, but rather is assuring us that because of the Holy Spirit, we are equipped to study on our own and to check to see if what we are being taught is consistent with the truth of Scripture.

    E. What is John's exhortation according to verse 28 and why?

    F. What family likeness will true children of God bear? (v. 29)

7. Explain how the purity of our mind regarding the truth of Christ affects our beauty to Him.

DAY 4

She Will Be Confident and Unashamed When Christ Returns

Pam and I sat on the dock dangling our feet into the waters of Lake Oswego on a summer day. Pam was a new Christian and was telling me that this new life she had received had some surprises! Intently, she said:

The first big surprise that Scripture revealed was that I was supposed to submit to my husband!"

I laughed. "What else has surprised you?"

Pam made a circle in the water with her foot. "You know what really blows me away?"

"Tell me!"

"That Jesus is coming back! I grew up in church, but I was never told that Jesus is coming back. Yet it's everywhere in the Scriptures! It gives me goose bumps to think about it, Dee. I want to be ready for Him. I don't want to be ashamed when He appears."

8. What do you learn about Jesus' return from the following passages?

   A. "They were looking intently up into the sky as he was going, when suddenly two men dressed in white stood beside them. 'Men of Galilee,' they said, 'why do you stand here looking into the sky? This same Jesus, who has been taken from you into heaven, will come back in the same way you have seen him go into heaven'" (Acts 1:10–11).

   B. "For the Lord himself will come down from heaven, with a loud command, with the voice of the archangel and with the trumpet call of God, and the dead in Christ will rise first. After that, we who are still alive and are left will be caught up together with them in the clouds to meet the Lord in the air. And so we will be there with the Lord forever" (1 Thess. 4:16–17).

   C. "Live deeply in Christ. Then we'll be ready for him when he appears, ready to receive him with open arms, with no cause for red-faced guilt or lame excuses when he arrives" (1 John 2:28 MSG).

9. When did you first realize Jesus was coming back? How does this truth impact your daily life?

10. As you look over the first two chapters of 1 John, what kind of choices will cause Christ to become more complete in you so that you will be a confident and radiant bride when He appears?

In your personal time now with God, pray through the below passages for your own character, asking God for the strength and grace to be like Him.

    A. 1 John 1:7

    B. 1 John 1:9

    C. 1 John 2:3

    D. 1 John 2:6

    E. 1 John 2:10

    F. 1 John 2:15–17

    G. 1 John 2:28

Can you say 1 John 2:22 by heart?

DAY 5

A Glorious Bride

I long to be a beautiful bride when Christ returns, but I fail every day! I am so thankful for the promise of 1 John 1:7–9, that if I walk in repentance He will be faithful to cleanse me and make me pure.

But there are also wonderful promises in 1 John of how we can *grow* in purity. Meditate again on what John Stott said:

> *Our love and our hatred not only reveal if we are in the light or the darkness, but actually contribute to the light or darkness in which we already are.* (*The Letters of John*, Eerdmans, 2000, p. 99)

Today you will see the many times John tells us that "as we choose something," Christ becomes complete in us.

11. Find the way Christ can become complete in you:

   A. 1 John 2:5

   B. 1 John 4:12

   C. 1 John 4:17

12. There are three symphonic manifestations in 1 John. See if you can write out a memory passage for each.

Walking in light ...

Walking in love ...

Walking in truth ...

On-the-Spot Action Assignment

Pass around a hat for women to put their names in to exchange secret sisters. Be faithful to pray for your secret sister and to show her love (such as encouraging notes, a loaf of homemade bread, or a bunch of wildflowers delivered by a co-conspirator!). You'll reveal your secret sisters the last week.

PRAYER TIME

Pray using popcorn prayer. Pray for each of you to cling to the original teaching, to be protected from false teaching, and to discern the red flags.

Prayers & Praises

_____

_____

_____

_____

_____

_____

_____

_____

_____

_____

_____

_____

_____

Six

The Distinctive Beauty of Calvary Love
1 John 3

As women, most of us have been gifted, by our Creator, to be nurturing. It's usually women who remember birthdays, organize family reunions, and respond to friends in pain with sympathetic tears. Even women who don't know the Lord often demonstrate this kind of love to their friends and family.

The difference I have seen in a woman who is abiding in Christ is that her love goes beyond a human response to a supernatural response. Like Christ, she responds to unkindness with kindness; she loves not just those who love her, but those who are hard to love; and she's alert, looking for ways to minister to those who are in spiritual, physcal, or emotional need. Lee Ezell tells of just such a woman who ministered to her during the darkest hour of her life.

Mom Croft had spotted Lee visiting her church. Lee was pregnant, carrying a child conceived in rape. After her pregnancy was discovered, Lee's mother cast her out of their home. Lonely and desperate, Lee tells of meeting Mom Croft.

> *After the service a great big woman with an equally big smile greeted me and said, "Where are you going to lunch, girl?" Lee followed Mom Croft and her husband to a tiny house just a half a block from the church.*

> *"Just moved here, didn't you?" she said as she started cooking eggs, grits, and biscuits.*

> *"Yes, how did you know?"*

> *"I can tell," she said with a twinkle in her eye. "Mom Croft can spot a lonely, hungry girl."*
> (*The Missing Piece*, Bantam, p. 50)

Lee moved in with the Crofts (who in their tiny house always found room for a "stray"). Because of Mom Croft's Christlike love, Lee experienced great healing and found the spiritual courage to carry her baby to term and to give her daughter to a loving Christian couple.

The third chapter of 1 John returns to the theme of love, and begins with the wonderful phrase "Behold, what manner of love the Father hath bestowed unto us!" (KJV). The Greek word for the phrase "what manner of" is *potapen*, which means "what country, race, or tribe?" It speaks of something foreign. It is not a natural kind of love but a supernatural kind. And those who are born of God and have the Holy Spirit should be habitually exhibiting this same kind of foreign supernatural love to others. Mom Croft did—and so can we—if we are abiding in Christ.

WARMUP

Share a time when someone was alert to your spiritual, emotional, or physical needs.

DAY 1
. . . .

She Rejoices in the "Foreign" Love of God

When I was a baby Christian, my husband was transferred to another city. When I heard the news, I called my sister Sally, who had led me to the Lord. "We're moving," I wept. "I can't believe we are leaving Seattle."

"Dee," my sister asked, "where is your real home?"

"Seattle!"

"No, Dee, your real home is in heaven. You are just sojourning down here. With His amazing love, God has reached down and made you one of His children. And just as Jesus was a sojourner, an alien on earth, so are you. Set your mind on things above, for your real life is hidden with Christ in God. One day Jesus is coming to take you home" (Col. 3:2–4).

As the third chapter of 1 John begins, John again is filled with awe at the amazing, "foreign" love of God. Then he proceeds to the mysterious thought that we are like this "foreign" God if we have been born of Him. We need to remember that we are strangers on this earth, our citizenship is in heaven, and our actions and our love should be very different from those who are not children of God.

70

In your personal quiet time, sing "Behold, What Manner of Love" (Hymns Index), and then spend a few moments in praise to God for His amazing love for you.

Begin memorizing 1 John 3:16:

This is how we know what love is: Jesus Christ laid down his life for us. And we ought to lay down our lives for our brothers.

Most of you know John 3:16, so this should be an easy reference to remember!

Read 1 John 3:1–3.

1. In verse 1, what are some of the words or phrases which capture John's awe at the love of God?

The Greek captures the idea that this love is not natural or usual, but actually foreign. How is God's love different from the kind of love that non-Christians have? Share a time when you were particularly aware of God's amazing love.

2. Just as God's love is a foreign kind of love, so are His children like "foreigners," people from another planet. Why is it that the people of the world fail to understand the people of God? (v. 1)

Read 1 Peter 2:9–12.

3. What similar thoughts do you see in this passage?

Though unbelievers may not understand believers, they will be drawn to God through the righteousness of believers. Was that true in your life? If so, share an example.

4. According to 1 John 3:2, what are we now?

5. What process will be completed and when, according to 1 John 3:2? What about this is mysterious to you?

6. What impact should all of the above truths have on our behavior? (1 John 3:3) What does this mean?

Read 1 John 3:4–10.

At first reading, John seems to say that the believer doesn't sin. However, that would not be consistent with 1 John 1:8. What he is saying is that if we have been born of God, we have God's nature. Therefore it would be inconsistent with the nature of God to be habitually turned toward sin the way an unbeliever is.

7. In each of the following sections, state the two thoughts John links together (this is true; therefore, this is also true):

   A. 1 John 3:5–6

   B. 1 John 3:7

   C. 1 John 3:8

   D. 1 John 3:9

8. What are two ways, according to verse 10, to discern who is a child of God and who is a child of the devil?

DAY 2

If We've Passed from Death to Life, We'll Love Each Other

When our daughter Sally was twelve, we adopted an adorable five- year-old girl from an orphanage in Korea. Sally experienced some Cain-like sibling rivalry at that time. Now as an adult, Sally shares this:

I was excited about getting Annie, until she arrived. Then when I saw all the attention move from me to her, envy welled up in my heart. James 3:16 tells us that where you have envy, you find disorder and every evil practice. That envy led to my being unkind to Annie, and to a deep depression for me—sleepless nights and miserable days.

At a Christian program one night, the speaker talked about the importance of keeping Christ on the throne of our lives, and God convicted me that I had allowed myself to take over that throne. I went forward for a recommitment and asked God to take out all the yuck I felt in my heart, and to step back on the throne of my life. He filled me with a love for Annie. Today I cannot imagine life without Annie—I love her so much. And my heart is filled not only with love, but also with joy!

9. Can you identify with the above story in any way?

John uses a powerful illustration from Genesis to demonstrate the truths about love he has been teaching.

10. In 1 John 3:11–12, what example does John give and what do you learn about Cain?

11. Read Genesis 4:1–15.

A. Describe Cain's emotions in verse 5. Why do you think he was feeling this way? (remember 1 John 3:12)

B. What two alternatives did God say were before Cain, and with what resulting consequences?

73

C. How does this exemplify what John has been teaching about light or darkness becoming more complete in you?

D. Which did Cain choose, and what happened?

E. List each time the word "brother" is spoken in this Genesis story. Do you see any significance in the repetition?

F. John applies this story to brothers and sisters in the Lord. What reasons can you give for this being particularly important to God? (See 1 John 3:14–15.)

G. Have you experienced disobedience leading to the enemy gaining a foothold on you? If so, share something about it.

H. Have you experienced obedience leading to greater strength in God? If so, share something about it.

12. What point is John making with the story of Cain? Is there an application for your life?

Continue learning your memory passage.

DAY 3

She Will Not "Snap Shut Her Heart" To Brethren in Need

There have been times when God has brought a "sister in need" across my path and my honest thought has been, *Lord, if I respond too warmly to her, I'll never be rid of her!* My natural response is to "snap shut my heart" or, as the *Scofield King James Version* translates it, "shutteth up his compassions."

My husband was different, however. He was always the one who wanted us to have someone in spiritual or emotional need move right in with us for a while. If they began to take advantage of us, then he would set boundaries, but he said he would always rather err on the side of being too giving than too stingy.

Christ did not shut up His compassions from us—He died for us when we were helpless sinners. As children of God, we must not shut up our compassions from one another.

Read 1 John 3:16–18.

13. What example defines true love in verse 16? How could you apply this verse to your life right now? Be specific.

14. How does John exhort us to express Calvary love in verses 17–18?

15. Share a time when your natural response was to "snap shut your heart" or to "shut up your compassions." Did you overcome that initial response or not? How did you then feel?

Jean Troup, the director of a shelter for homeless women in Maryland, shared this in an interview with me:

I think the Gospel demonstrates that God wants us to get involved with those in need because God could have just snapped His fingers and saved us, but instead He died on a cross. It always hurts to get involved, but I believe that is what He has called us to do.... The Lord has definitely converted me from a sheltered lifestyle to getting out and dealing with peoples' hurts and desperate situations from a faith perspective.

16. What hurting people are you aware of in your church, neighborhood, or life sphere?

Is God impressing a plan of action on your heart? If so, what?

DAY 4

• •

Not Just in Word, but in Deed

It's so easy to say we forgive, we care, or we will pray … but the genuineness of our faith is proven when we follow through. Seeking to please that audience of One results in loving not just in word, but in deed and in truth.

17. What does 1 John 3:18 say?

18. Read James 2:14–20

   A. What question does he ask in verse 14? Compare this to John's statement in 1 John 3:18.

   B. What illustration does James give in James 2:15–16?

   C. How about in James 2:19?

   D. What does it mean to say "faith without works is useless"?

19. Consider:

   A. Is there a wall between you and a sister or brother in Christ? Have you done everything you can to humble yourself and, with no excuses for yourself, to go and make peace?

   B. Is there someone in your life God has brought across your path who is in genuine need? Have you sought God on how you might respond and then obeyed?

DAY 5

. . . .

A Habitually Loving Heart Is a Heart at Rest

In Amy Carmichael's book *If*, each page has a sentence describing Calvary love, such as:

> *If I fear to hold another to the highest because it is so much easier to avoid doing so, then I know nothing of Calvary love.*

> *If I can enjoy a joke at the expense of another; if I can in any way slight another in conversation, or even in thought, then I know nothing of Calvary love.*

Elisabeth Elliot said each sentence seared her, and each time the Holy Spirit said, "Guilty!" (*Bright Legacy*, Servant, p. 23).

That is the way each of us tends to feel after reading 1 John 3:16–18. We have fallen short of Calvary love. Our failures rise up, and our hearts condemn us!

20. But John has a solution for a condemning heart:

A. What does John tell us to do in 1 John 3:18?

B. What will be the result? (1 John 3:19)

C. There are tender hearts that may still be anxious. How does John address them in 1 John 3:20?

> *However firmly grounded the Christian's assurance is, his heart may sometimes need reassurance.... Sometimes the accusations of our "conscience" will be true accusations, and sometimes they will be false, inspired by "the accuser of our brethren" (Rev. 12:10).... Our conscience is by no means infallible; its condemnation may often be unjust. We can, therefore, appeal from our conscience to God who is greater and more knowledgeable. Indeed, he knows all things, including our secret motives and deepest resolves, and, it is implied, will be more merciful toward us than our own heart. (John Stott, The Epistles of John, Intervarsity Press, pp. 145–46)*

D. It is important to breathe truth to ourselves when our hearts condemn us, for we have an enemy who breathes lies, telling us we can't really be forgiven. He haunts us with past sins that have long been cast by God into the deepest ocean. If you are being accused, what truths from God's Word could you use to send the enemy fleeing?

If you don't "feel" forgiven, then stand on the promises of God's Word.

21. What is the evidence that God is for us, according to 1 John 3:22?

22. What is another way that we can grow in our confidence that we are, truly, His children? (1 John 3:23)

23. What do you think you will remember best from this chapter?

PRAYER TIME

Take prayer requests and then pray using popcorn prayer. Close your prayer time by singing "Behold, What Manner of Love."

Prayers &
Praises

_____

_____

_____

_____

_____

_____

_____

_____

_____

_____

_____

_____

Seven

The Beauty of Overcoming Love

1 John 4

When our son John was sixteen, he went through a period of rebellion and was befriended by a group of boys who drank. My husband and I became more strict with John and changed his curfew. But he'd sneak out of his bedroom window after we were asleep. It was a terrible time for all of us. John was experiencing the consequences of sin, and my husband and I always feared the worst—a phone call saying there'd been an accident. My sister Sally prayed and fasted with me that Satan's hold on John would be broken. "Greater is He that is in you, Dee," Sally said, "than the one who is in the world" (1 John 4:4).

My mentor, Shirley Ellis, reminded me of God's faithfulness. And she talked to me about the importance of showing John love, even though I was angry with his behavior. A beautiful word picture of the power of love occurs in Song of Solomon 8:7 where we are told "Many waters cannot quench love; rivers cannot wash it away." The picture I had was of my surly teenage son throwing buckets of water on my love, and yet, being unable to quench it! And so as God persisted in loving me, I persisted in loving John. I played chess with him. I gave him backrubs. And I prayed and fasted for him.

John came back to God and to us in repentance one morning. Since that day twenty years ago, John has walked closely with God, loving and serving Him.

When we love with God's love, we overcome the Evil One, not only for this generation, but also for the generations to come. I now see John's four children walking in the truth. Greater is He that is in us than He that is in the world! When you love others with the love of God, darkness flees, hearts are mended, and children yet to be born are given hope.

WARMUP

Ask group members to finish this sentence: When someone returns my unkindness with kindness, I feel...

DAY I

She Discerns the Spirits

The percussion instruments now take the lead, reminding us of the importance of walking in the truth. Truth and love are like the balanced wings of an airplane—for truth without love is merciless, and love without truth is a crippling enabler.

Peter describes our enemy the devil as "a roaring lion" prowling around looking for someone to devour (1 Peter 5:8). "Be alert!" the apostle warns. The devil wants to rob us (and our children) of our joy and fruitfulness. And he is not only inspiring the cults and false teachers, but you can find him in schools, in movies, even on "Oprah." And the world is listening to him, making his books, movies, and music big business! Jesus tells us that the devil can disguise himself as an angel of light. How then are we to recognize him?

Read 1 John 4:1–6.

1. Circle or note how many times in this passage John uses the phrases "is from," "are from," "is not from," and "are not from." John wants us to recognize the source of everything we read, see, or hear.

Read 1 John 4:1–6 (MSG):

> *My dear friends, don't believe everything you hear. Carefully weigh and examine what people tell you. Not everyone who talks about God comes from God. There are a lot of lying preachers loose in the world.*

> *Here's how you test for the genuine Spirit of God. Everyone who confesses openly his faith in Jesus Christ—the Son of God, who came as an actual flesh-and-blood person—comes from God and belongs to God. And everyone who refuses to confess faith in Jesus has nothing in common with God. This is the spirit of antichrist that you heard was coming. Well, here it is, sooner than we thought!*

> *My dear children, you come from God and belong to God. You have already won a big victory over those false teachers, for the Spirit in you is far stronger than anything in the world. These people belong to the Christ-denying world. They talk the world's language*

and the world eats it up. But we come from God and belong to God. Anyone who knows God understands us and listens. The person who has nothing to do with God will, of course, not listen to us. This is another test for telling the Spirit of Truth from the spirit of deception.

2. John gives two distinguishing tests to discern the spirits. Describe them:

    A. 1 John 4:2–3

"Come in the flesh" refers to the Incarnation, which means Jesus is God.

    B. 1 John 4:5–6

3. A speaker who possesses the Spirit of God and a speaker who possesses the spirit of the antichrist will stimulate a predictable reaction from an audience that contains both unbelievers and believers. Describe a time when you have seen this happen (a classroom, observing a talk show audience, etc.).

John is saying here that we must be gentle and winsome when we present the message of God. However, even when we are gentle and winsome, rejection should not surprise us (1 John 3:13).

4. With the tests of 1 John 4:2–3 and 5–6 in mind, give an example of a philosophy, book, or TV show that passes these tests and another that fails these tests.

    A. What example(s) can you give that shows the Spirit of God? How does it pass the above tests?

    B. What example(s) can you give that shows the spirit of the antichrist? How does it fail the above tests?

Memorize 1 John 4:4 (KJV), which corresponds to the song in your Hymns Index:

Ye are of God, little children, and have overcome them: because greater is he that is in you, than he that is in the world.

DAY 2
....

She Overcomes the Spirit of the Antichrist

When Satan waged a war for our son John, my husband and I joined forces with friends to pray fervently for him. When the battle was fiercest, we clung to this promise: "He who is in you is greater than he who is in the world" (1 John 4:4).

Today you will discover ways to wage spiritual battle and overcome the spirit of the antichrist—not only in your own mind and heart, but also in the minds and hearts of the children to whom God has entrusted you.

Read Ephesians 6:12–18.

5. Describe the struggle (v. 12). How have you seen this spiritual battle in your life? How have you seen this in the lives of the children to whom God has entrusted you? If you are not a parent, how have you seen this in the lives of your friends, nieces, or nephews?

6. Describe the clothing a beautiful woman wears to be an "overcomer." Explain in practical terms how you could better use the items found in each of the following passages.

   A. Ephesians 6:13–15

   B. Ephesians 6:16

   C. Ephesians 6:17

   D. Ephesians 6:18

Action Assignment

Choose one of the following actions, and do it today or tomorrow! At your small group, you will be asked what you did.

Watch a secular TV program with a child. Ask him or her afterward: What were the Christian values? What were the values that opposed Christ?

Pray through Colossians 1:9–10 for a child you care about.

Don't forsake the dinner hour! There is a reason Jesus often spoke truths to his disciples over the breaking of bread. Determine to eat together as a family nearly every night, and after those meals, read aloud from C. S. Lewis's Narnia books, *Anne of Green Gables*, *Jane Eyre*, or a biography of a great Christian.

When you've completed the Action Assignment, record what you did along with any comments you might have.

DAY 3

She Overcomes with Love

When our daughter Sally was a seventh grader, an eighth-grade girl chose her to be the target of her jokes. One night Sally tearfully said, "When I went into computer lab today, Amber tripped me! I sprawled all over the floor. She and her friends laughed hysterically."

After comforting my daughter (and resisting the urge to personally strangle Amber!), we talked about the kind of love which overcomes evil. Romans 12:19–21 says:

> *Do not take revenge, my friends, but leave room for God's wrath, for it is written: "It is mine to avenge; I will repay," says the Lord. One the contrary: "If your enemy is hungry, feed him; if he is thirsty, give him something to drink. In doing this, you will heap burning coals on his head." Do not be overcome by evil, but overcome evil with good.*

With a plan and all of my prayer support behind her, Sally entered the computer lab the next day and walked right up to Amber and said: "Amber, I saw your tennis scores in the paper. Good job!"

Sally came running home from school that night. Breathlessly, she said, "Mom! It worked! Amber blushed when I said that, and then, really meekly, she said: 'Thanks.' And later, when I passed her in the hall, she said: 'Hi, Sally.'"

The hardest time to love someone is when they don't deserve it. We certainly didn't deserve to have Jesus die for us, yet He did. Now He calls us to give the same kind of love to others.

Read 1 John 4:7–11.

7. What reason does John give us for showing overcoming love to one another? Can you think of a time when you showed or were shown overcoming love? If so, share something about it.

The best translation of 1 John 4:8 is not "God is love," for that could lead you to the inaccurate idea that God is an abstraction. The Greek really says, "God as to His nature is love" (Kenneth Wuest, *Word Studies in the Greek New Testament*, Eerdmans, pp. 163–64).

8. Look up the words atonement and propitiation. What do you learn? How did Jesus make it possible for God to be favorably disposed toward us?

9. What conclusion does John come to in verse 11? Is there a child, neighbor, or relative to whom God is prompting you to show overcoming love? If so, whom? What will you do?

DAY 4

Evidence of the Spirit

Everyone who has received Christ has received the fullness of the Spirit. We cannot see the Holy Spirit, but we can see evidence of Him at work in our lives. Likewise, others cannot see God, but they can see evidence of God in the love of believers.

My first encounter with a believer that I can clearly remember was my fifth-grade teacher in a public school. I remember Miss Kolander as being astonishingly beautiful, with flaming red hair and stylish clothes. But I know it was the love and wisdom in her that set her apart from the other teachers. She really cared about us and listened intently to us. She wrote encouraging notes on our papers. She set boundaries and kept them, loving with truth. She disciplined most strongly for swearing, saying simply, "God is holy and He died and rose again for us," so she would discipline anyone who took His name in vain.

She insisted on respect, not only for God, but also for herself and our peers, because loving one another was the second greatest commandment! She introduced the class to the idea that sex within marriage was beautiful and God's good idea! She looked to the Lord, and she was radiant. She caused her students to be drawn to God for the evidence of the Spirit was so strong in her.

Read 1 John 4:12–18.

10. What similar thought is repeated in verses 12 and 17?

11. Share about "a woman of beauty" that you know in whom God's Spirit is particularly evident. What do you see?

12. Have you experienced more of the presence of God when you have lived out His love? If so, share something about it.

John repeatedly emphasizes that if we have some fears concerning the genuineness of our conversion, we can set those fears to rest through living out God's love. Obedience leads to "confidence!" Since confidence is the opposite of fear, this is the "mature love" that drives out fear.

13. According to the following verses, what kind of behavior will make us confident?

    A. 1 John 2:28

    B. 1 John 3:18–19

    C. 1 John 4:16–17

14. Judgment day will be a day of shame and terror for the wicked. How should the child of God feel? Why? (1 John 4:16–18)

John Stott explains the phrase "as He is (i.e., Christ), so are we in this world": "Jesus is God's beloved Son, in whom He is well pleased; we too are God's children and the objects of His favor" (*The Epistles of John*, Tyndale, p. 169).

DAY 5

Mature Love Drives Out Hate

How do you react when a relative or friend hurts your feelings? The most natural response in the world to pain is withdrawal. But God does not call us to be natural—He calls us to be supernatural.

Read 1 John 4:19–21.

15. Why should we love? (v. 19)

16. What strong statements does John make? (v. 20)

17. Write the *natural* response in the following situations, and then record the *supernatural* response.

   A. You get along well with the other fifth-floor employees, a new girl is hired who is a bit "irregular" and not well liked.

   The natural response:

   The supernatural response:

   B. A good friend hurts your feelings.

   The natural response:

   The supernatural response:

   C. Your son marries a girl you don't particularly like.

   The natural response:

   The supernatural response:

18. Is God speaking to you through this lesson? If so, how?

PRAYER TIME

Pray, using the last answer as a guide for popcorn prayer. Then close by singing "Greater Is He."

Prayers & Praises

_____

_____

_____

_____

_____

_____

_____

_____

_____

_____

_____

Eight

A Woman of Beauty Is Confident

1 John 5

Beautiful models walk tall, holding their shoulders back with confidence in their step. Likewise, we as believers should have the beauty of confidence, for we have a very big God who loves us.

In a women's Bible study made up primarily of beginners, the women were inhibited toward praying together. But then something happened. During a study, a mother began to weep as she shared her frustrations about her disrespectful teenager.

"She told me she hates me and she hopes I'll die!" Lynn wept. Sympathetically, the women next to her hugged her. We spontaneously surrounded her chair and began to pray for her:

"Father, please give Lynn wisdom with her daughter."

"Yes, Lord. And please melt Molly's heart."

"Lord, please have Lynn's husband intervene when Molly is disrespectful."

"Yes, Lord, I agree."

The next week Lynn came into the study brimming with news: "Last week, after you prayed," she said excitedly, "I asked Molly to take out the trash after supper. She ran up to her room and said, 'No! I'm not your slave!' My husband calmly followed her and brought her back down. Firmly he told her she was not to talk to me like that. Then he had her take out the trash. Molly and I were both stunned because he'd never intervened like that before. Suddenly I realized, *It's because those women prayed!"*

That week the inhibitions to prayer came down. Women were willing to say simple sentence prayers, and to say, "I agree, Lord!" And we began to see things happen. Oh, the joy of overcoming faith!

John ends this letter much as he began it: We belong to a real God! This is no fairy tale! Jesus is real! The Spirit is real! And the woman who realizes this is plugged into a power that can overcome the world!

Our confidence is not in ourselves, but in the One who created the world, opened the Red Sea for His children, loved us enough to die for us, and was raised from the dead. He lives in us, empowers us through His Spirit, bends down and answers our prayers, and is as near as our very breath.

WARMUP

Briefly share an example of answered prayer from your life that had an impact on you. What did that cause you to believe about God?

DAY I

Her Faith Is Not Burdensome Because It Overcomes the World!

I've just spent an evening with ten friends who are all strong women in the Lord. Though we may have come weary or even sad, our shared laughter caused our endorphins to rise significantly. We prayed for the woman facing a custody battle and for the young mom soon to give birth. We encouraged one another through the singing of hymns and the sharing of answered prayer. We left feeling strong, knowing we belonged to a mighty God who overcomes the world.

Read 1 John 5:1–5.

1. According to verse 1, what are two consequences of believing that Jesus is the Christ?

2. Why is it logical that if you love the father you love the child too?

Why is it logical that if you love God you obey His commands?

3. One of the reasons the commands of God are not burdensome to a believer is because they empower her to overcome the world. Review some of the commands in 1 John that can help you overcome the problems or sorrows of the world (1:7, 9; 2:15–17; 4:12).

Share personally and specifically how one of the above commands has given you victory and joy.

Memorize 1 John 5:13

I write these things to you who believe in the name of the Son of God so that you may know that you have eternal life.

DAY 2

Her Faith Is Based on Reliable Evidence

Most people have a longing for spiritual reality, and that has led them in many directions. The late Paul Little has said that it is crucial to examine the object of our faith, for our faith is only as reliable as the object in which it is placed. For example, if a man believes with his whole heart that his faulty parachute will take him safely to the ground, he will still crash. What matters is not the sincerity of his faith, but the reliability of the object in which it is placed. How reliable an object is Jesus?

Read 1 John 5:6–10.

4. How did Jesus come by water at the beginning of His earthly ministry? What evidence was given then for trusting Him? (Matt. 3:13–17)

How did Jesus come by blood at the end of His earthly ministry? What evidence was given then for trusting Him? (List things such as fulfilled prophecies and supernatural events. A few examples are in Matt. 27:3–10, 50–54; 28:1–10.)

We are born again, not by the reasoning of man, but by the power of the Holy Spirit. The

Spirit, however, may teach an individual, showing her the overwhelming evidence. Sara Groves sings, "I don't claim to have found the truth, but that the truth found me!"

As a twenty-one-year-old wife and mother, I thought about the people I knew who didn't believe. Were they right? Was I surrendering to a fairy tale? But, (and I am so thankful) the Spirit had hold of me, opening my eyes, showing me the overwhelming evidence: the hundreds of fulfilled prophecies, the evidence for the resurrection, and the changed lives of the apostles. Then, the day I knelt in surrender to the Lord, He confirmed my faith in two dramatic ways: He took a burden from my back that I didn't even know I'd been carrying, and He took the blinders from my eyes that I didn't even know I'd been wearing. Jesus truly was who He claimed to be—God!

5. Now John mentions this third testimony, that of the Holy Spirit, reminding us of Romans 8:16: "The Spirit himself testifies with our spirit that we are God's children." In what ways has God's Spirit testified to you that you do, indeed, belong to Him?

6. Why is the person who refuses to believe not given further testimony?

DAY 3

Knowing We Have Eternal Life!

As a new believer I had a bumper sticker that said, "I'm bound for the promised land." A friend asked me what that meant, and I told her, "It means that I am confident of heaven." Her raised eyebrows caused me to explain. "I am confident, not because I feel that I am worthy, because I'm not. For years I completely ignored God and lived for myself. And even now, though I've given my life to Christ, I fail Him every day. I am still so unworthy. But I'm forgiven. Salvation is based on my trust in Christ's payment for my sin on the cross. That is why I know I have eternal life."

In your personal quiet time, sing praises for God's amazing grace. (Suggestions: "Behold, What Manner of Love," "Amazing Grace," or "And Can It Be?")

Can you say 1 John 5:13 by heart?

Read 1 John 5:11–13.

7. What black-and-white statement does John make in verse 12?

What is one of the purposes of John's letter, according to verse 13?

What does it mean to you that you can know—not hope—that you have eternal life?

John's letter reflects a balance that is often missing in both mainline and evangelical churches. Whereas mainline churches may fail to emphasize that we are saved by faith, evangelical churches may fail to emphasize that genuine faith results in a transformed life. If we do not obey God's Word, if we do not love our brother, if we are continually sinning, then we have reason to doubt that we have genuine saving faith. John tells us repeatedly that our confidence in our salvation will grow as we see these evidences in our life, not because they save us, but because they demonstrate that God's Spirit lives in us.

8. Do you see the following evidences in your life for saving faith? If so, share a specific example.

   A. 1 John 2:1

   B. 1 John 2:3

   C. 1 John 2:9–10

DAY 4
Knowing He Hears Us

In *What Happens When Women Pray,* Evelyn Christenson tells how God transformed eight gripers (the tired, spiritual-life chairwomen of her church!) into eight women who learned to pray together. The result? Their church was absolutely revitalized! Not only that, it was contagious, as sisters across America came to Mrs. Christenson's prayer seminars. When one woman was invited by her sister to a seminar, she thought, *A prayer seminar? What good will it do? I have prayed and prayed and it hasn't done any good.* She and her family were suffering from financial and health problems, and she doubted more prayer would help. But she went.

At that seminar, 1 John 5:14–15 changed her heart. "Up to that point," she said, "I had not asked for God's will. I could only see what I wanted to happen." But that day, as she stood with four Christian sisters, she prayed: "Lord, I want your perfect will for me and my family."

At that moment she felt the load lift. Nine months later she said, "I cannot begin to tell you of the peace I have in my heart. My husband's business debts are not all cleared up as yet, but God is moving. The burden is lifted. My health has improved tremendously." Her prayers, she now believes, went unanswered before because she had not asked God for His will.

Read 1 John 5:14–15.

9. What confidence can we have in approaching God? What prerequisite is given in verse 14? What does this mean? What other prerequisite is given in 1 John 3:22?

10. What is an earnest prayer desire of your heart? How might you apply the above prerequisites to this?

Read 1 John 5:16–17.

This is, perhaps, the most difficult passage in 1 John. The most convincing explanation I have heard for "sin unto death" is made by John Stott, who says, in the context of the whole letter, that sin is the rejection of Christ. Throughout the letter we are warned against counterfeits who claim to be brothers, but in reality have rejected Christ (*Epistles of John,* Tyndale, p. 190). We cannot pray for them to be saved apart from Christ, but we can pray for genuine brothers and sisters who have sinned in other ways, and God will give them life.

DAY 5

Jesus Will Keep You, but Keep Yourselves from Idols!

A study of the Greek words meaning "keep" in the closing passage of 1 John reveals the concept of "guard." God will guard His children against Satan, who is prowling like a roaring lion. But we have a responsibility to guard our hearts from anything that would get between us and God. This requires diligence, just as an actual guard must not fall asleep on the job!

To begin your personal quiet time, sing "Behold, What Manner of Love" (Hymns Index).

Read 1 John 5:18–21.

11. Describe how the word "keep" is used in verse 18. How does this make you feel? Think back and remember a time when God kept you from the snares of Satan. What was the snare, and how did God keep you?

12. What responsibility is given to us in verse 21? What are some of the idols that tend to get between you and God?

The word "keep" in verse 21 may have the connotation in the Greek of guarding through isolation. This is contrary to the way the world thinks, for the world encourages exposure. Those who isolate themselves from certain books, movies, sexual expressions, material pleasures … are labeled as "narrow." And yet here, God tells us to guard our hearts, to isolate ourselves from certain influences. It reminds me of Titus 2, where women are told to be "keepers at home" or to "guard over the hearts of their children."

Though we have great liberty in Christ, that liberty is not to be an excuse for sin. The challenges are greater for today's mothers; television, video games, the Internet, schools, and our children's peers bring all kinds of corrupting influences into our children's lives. God will not lead all of us in the same way, but we all must seriously endeavor to "keep ourselves from idols," from anything that would come between us and God or between the children in our care and God.

13. How is God leading you to guard your heart? To guard the hearts of those in your care?

14. Look at the three "we knows" in 1 John 5:18–20. What do believers know? And how does this make them different from those in the world?

15. What has God impressed on your heart from this study or the discussion of 1 John 5?

PRAYER TIME

Pray using question 9 as a guide for popcorn prayer. Remember to ask for God's will and to make sure there is nothing between you and God when you pray.

Prayers & Praises

_____

_____

_____

_____

_____

_____

_____

_____

_____

_____

_____

_____

Nine

The Beauty Is Passed On
2 John

Thirty years ago in Ohio, I had the joy of being used by God to lead a young mother of three small children to the Lord. Jesus turned Lee Petno's life around, and the change was so evident that her husband, upon meeting me, said, "Are you the one who is responsible for the wonderful change in my wife?"

I laughed and said, "No, Jesus did that!"

"Really!" he said, astonished. Soon after that he, too, put his trust in Christ.

Twelve years ago, I flew back to Ohio for the wedding of Lee's daughter. The wedding was distinctively Christian with both the bride and groom expressing a heartfelt faith. Today they are in full-time mission work. At the reception, I visited with Lee's now grown sons and heard them express their passion for serving Christ. I met grandchildren who already seemed different from children in the world because of their faith in a living God.

When I returned home I wrote Lee a letter that expressed a joy similar to that found in 2 John. How it thrilled my heart to see her and her husband continuing in the truth, and to see their children and grandchildren walking in the truth as well! What an affirmation of the power of the Spirit to change lives from one generation to the next.

John writes to the elect lady, and commentators are divided on whether this is a woman who had been a leader in the early church, or whether this is a symbolic way of addressing a church. I am increasingly persuaded that he is addressing someone specific—that is the most natural way to interpret John's words. He also closes with greetings from her "sister," another indication this is personal. Some have thought he might be writing to Martha of Bethany. But whether she is an individual woman with biological children or whether he is writing to a church with spiritual children, there is joy in seeing the next generation living wholeheartedly for Christ. When the love of Jesus is vibrant in an individual or in a church, the beauty is passed on. Now John urges the lady and her children to continue in love, and also to guard their hearts against the abundant anti-Christian propaganda.

WARMUP

Share a time when you felt joy because you saw your own children or the children of someone you loved walking in the truth. Why did it give you joy?

DAY I

The Beauty of Seeing Our Children Walk in Truth

Proverbs tells us of the great joy that comes to the parent of a wise child (Prov. 10:1; 29:3). In my life, nothing has given me more joy than seeing our grown children walk in the truth. Women, whether they are biological mothers or spiritual mothers (and hopefully we are all the latter), experience great joy when they find their children walking in the truth. My figure and my skin are not what they once were, but there is a beauty that cannot fade, and that unfading beauty can be passed on to my children, to my children's children, and to children yet to be born.

Second John reiterates the beauty secrets of 1 John: love, truth, and light. Read through 2 John in its entirety; then read 2 John 1–4 again.

1. Note how many times John uses the word "truth" in this opening. When Jesus prayed for future believers in John 17:17, He prayed, "Sanctify them by the truth; your word is truth." With this in mind, specifically imagine some ways that it would be evident that individuals had not just intellectually accepted the truth, but had welcomed it in their hearts.

2. What factors do you think contribute significantly to helping children walk in the truth?

   My parents surrounded me with the gospel and nestled me in their love. I often happened in on my father as he sat alone with the Bible, tears streaming down his cheeks at the beauty of some revelation. In our home, prayer was a natural response to problems and crises as well as good news and celebrations. My parents were verbal about their rela-

tionship with God, with each other, with us children, and with others. (Gloria Gaither, *Today's Christian Woman,* Sept/Oct 1991, p. 48)

3. How did John pray for his spiritual children in verse 3?

Dr. James Dobson tells of a letter he received from his father which affected him profoundly. His father wrote:

I have observed that the greatest delusion is to suppose that our children will be devout Christians simply because their parents have been or that any of them will enter into life in any other way than through the valley of deep travail of prayer and faith.... But this prayer demands time, time that cannot be given if it is all signed and conscripted and laid on the altar of career ambition. (Rolf Zettersten, *Dr. Dobson: Turning Hearts Toward Home,* Word, p. 93)

On-the-Spot Action Assignment

Spend some time in prayer for your biological or spiritual children. Pray through Colossians 1:9–12 and 2 John 3 for them.

Begin memorizing 2 John 9.

Anyone who runs ahead and does not continue in the teaching of Christ does not have God; whoever continues in the teaching has both the Father and the Son.

DAY 2

Beauty Secret #1: Love One Another

If we want our children to walk in the truth, it is vital that we show them love. *In Faithful Parents, Faithful Kids* (Tyndale, p. 20), Mike Yorkey and Greg Johnson continually stress, "Behavior is important, but relationship is the bull's-eye." If I have a good relationship with someone, if I know they love me, I want to please them. And yet it seems so many parents (and spiritual parents!) have lost sight of this. They fail to show their children love, to affirm them, to spend time with them, and yet still expect them to listen to hard truths.

Read 2 John 5–6.

4. John repeats Christ's command that we "walk in love." What does this mean? If you are doing this guide in a small group, how might you better "walk in love" toward one another?

Action Assignment

Ask your children (or spiritual children) which of the following is their favorite way of receiving love.

Words of encouragement

Physical touch

Acts of service

Gifts

Spending time together

Then, endeavor to love one of your children, this week, in his favorite way to be loved. What do you plan to do?

5. Share your favorite way of receiving love. (Be particularly alert to your secret sister's favorite way of receiving love!)

Action Assignment

This week show your secret sister love according to her favorite way of receiving love.

Finish memorizing 2 John 9.

Anyone who runs ahead and does not continue in the teaching of Christ does not have God; whoever continues in the teaching has both the Father and the Son.

DAY 3

Beauty Secret #2: Guard Your Heart from Lies

In John's day, deceivers were coming to believers and offering a "new and improved" religion. Instead of presenting the simplicity of the gospel, they had added to it, twisted it, and said it was better! The same telltale sign is evident in today's cults. Also, many religions claim to have God, but they do not want Christ. Or, they have redefined Christ, stripping Him of His power and authority. John says here that if you do not have Christ, you do not have God.

Read 2 John 7–11.

6. Find the marks of a deceiver in verses 7 and 9.

7. What strong statement does John make in verse 9 about the person who does not continue in the teachings of Christ?

Denying that Jesus came in the flesh was denying the incarnation, that deity became man. They denied that Christ was God. John Stott says,

> *Many today want God without Jesus Christ. They say they believe in God, but see no necessity for Jesus. Or they want to bring non-Christian religions on to a level with Christianity, as alternative roads to God.... John refers sarcastically to their claim. They had indeed 'gone ahead.' They had advanced so far that they had left God behind them!* (*The Epistles of John,* Tyndale, p. 211)

8. It's popular today, as in John's day, to be religious but not to embrace Jesus. What warnings does John give to us in verses 8, 10–11?

In John's day, the practice of hospitality was so habitual that people seldom stayed in inns, and the inns that did exist were dirty and run-down. Therefore, missionaries almost always stayed in homes. John is telling believers that if they support false missionaries in this way, they are participating in their evil work.

This passage has sometimes been interpreted to not allow the occasional cult member who visits to come into your home. Many Christians are simply rude to these people. Though we certainly should guard our hearts, we have no permission here to be rude. Rudeness certainly won't win them, and neither will quarrels. When someone has been deceived (whether it is a cult member, a prodigal child, or an unbelieving coworker), arguments only heighten their defense. But love, kindness, and a humble testimony of Christ's power in our life may break down those walls.

My older sister Sally has been a mentor to me in dealing with cult members, having had success in talking to them. Recently I followed her example and asked two Mormon girls who came to my door how they had been treated by Christians. When the younger indicated that the receptions had varied, I apologized for my brothers and sisters. I briefly shared my testimony and prayed for all of us, that we would know the truth and that the truth would set us free. I could tell by their response that they were surprised by my warmth. I didn't affirm their faith, but neither was I rude to them. I prayed after they left, as Paul exhorts us to do, that God might open their eyes and free them from the devil who had captured them to do his will.

Read 2 Timothy 2:23–26.

9. What principles are given here for discussions with those who do not accept the claims of Christ? Find everything you can.

10. How will you respond to someone you love who has "run ahead," rejecting the Jesus of the Bible? Or, how will you respond in love and truth to the cult members who may approach you? Describe what you won't do and what you will do.

Can you say 2 John 9 by heart?

DAY 4

Beauty Secret #3: Keep Yourself Pure from Anti-Christian Propaganda in Mass Media

David Mains, who was a popular radio preacher for many years with a program called "Chapel of the Air," has pointed out that in John's day false teaching was limited to false missionaries, but today anti-Christian propaganda has multiplied through mass media. John's warnings should sound loudly in our ears when we think about all the ways media can come into our homes and influence us and our loved ones.

For one writing project I did research to see if there were any common variables among women who were walking in the truth and who had raised children who were walking in the truth. One of my most significant discoveries was that women who were leading radically transformed Christian lives severely limited their time with TV, and they spent that time instead listening to Christian music, Christian radio, and reading Scripture and Christian books. And from an early age, they helped their children do likewise. They usually owned a television (but often just one), but limited its use.

Review 2 John 4 and 7–11.

11. Do you see a connection between verse 4 and the warning in verses 7–11? In your own life? In the lives of the next generation? If so, share something about it.

David Mains sees a false religion sweeping North America and much of the world, dominating mass media. He says:

> *This sinister force I'm describing rejects Christ totally and ridicules those who speak on His behalf. It befriends other religions, but uniquely HATES the Son of God and all He represents.... This religion preaches a morality that not only opposes biblical Christianity but attacks many traditional standards of morality.... This is not just secular humanism. That name is too neutral. What is it? It is the aggressive, blatant, powerful, growing end-time religion of the Antichrist.* ("The Religion of Antichrist," pamphlet published by the Chapel of the Air)

12. Have you made a conscious effort to limit the ways anti-Christian propaganda comes into your home? Or into your heart? If you have had some success, share what you have done with the group.

13. How might a mother decrease the anti-Christian propaganda that comes into her children's' hearts and increase the truth they are exposed to?

> *By the time Billy Graham was ten, he'd memorized many passages of Scripture and all 107 articles in the Shorter Catechism. "We had Bible reading and prayer right after supper," his mother said. "We all got down on our knees and prayed, yes we did, sometimes for twenty to thirty minutes." Every Sunday afternoon Mrs. Graham would collect the children around the radio to listen to Charles Fuller's "Old Fashioned Revival Hour."* (Marshall Frady, *Billy Graham*, Little, Brown, & Co., p. 48)

DAY 5

Beauty Secret #4: Keep Your Light Shining

We can't stay in touch with everyone who has been dear to us, and God hasn't called us to maintain a Christmas card list of two hundred people. But there are some He is calling us to follow-up on, even from afar. John (and other New Testament writers) continued to let their light shine, not just to those nearby, but to those who lived faraway, especially their spiritual children. The model of the New Testament is:

Continued prayer

Continued letter writing (thank God for email!)

Occasional visits, as the Lord permits

On-the-Spot Action Assignment

Ask God whom He is leading you to stay in contact with. There may be some whom you influenced for the Lord who need follow-up and encouragement. There may be some beautiful women to whom your soul is knit, who have strengthened you, and you them, in Christ. Tend to those friendships, for they are more precious than gold. Are there children or siblings who need to know you care?

14. List the names God impresses on your heart. Then consider what He might have you do. If your list is too long, you will have trouble doing well, so plead with Him for discernment.

Read 2 John 12–13.

15. What does John tell the recipient of this letter in verse 12? What is the value of face-to-face visits over letters?

Kenneth Wuest observes that the sight of people's faces appeals to one's heart and softens one's speech, and often our judgment of them is modified. He tells of how Dr. Dale of Birmingham looked with disfavor on Mr. Moody until he went to hear him. "He regarded him ever after with profound respect, and considered that he had a right to preach the Gospel, 'because he could never speak of a lost soul without tears in his eyes'" (*Word Studies in the New Testament,* Eerdmans, pp. 208–209).

16. Do you have some long-distance friends or family members who have endeavored to remain close to you? How have they done it and what has it meant to you?

17. What do you think you will remember from 2 John that will make a difference in your life?

Remember that next week you will be revealing your secret sisters. You may wish to plan a special luncheon or refreshments.

PRAYER TIME

Take prayer requests, then pray using popcorn prayer.

Prayers & Praises

_____

_____

_____

_____

_____

_____

_____

_____

_____

_____

_____

_____

_____

_____

Ten

The Beauty of Hospitality
3 John

When my husband Steve was seeking a Christian medical practice, one of our visits took us to Iowa and a group of Mennonite doctors. The wife of one of the doctors invited me over to lunch on the spur of the moment. As I drove up to a compact ranch home, I wondered if I had scribbled down the wrong address (don't doctors usually have big houses?). But I knew I was at the right home when Margie opened the door, looking cheerful and eager to meet me. Margie took my coat and I found myself talking easily as her thoughtful questions coaxed me on. My eyes wandered over their living room. The grass-cloth and pictures from Algeria reminded me that they had spent years in a mission hospital there. The room had warmth and character; its inexpensive simplicity was refreshing.

We sat down to a nicely set table and had Campbell's soup and canned peaches. Short notice didn't stop Margie from inviting me for lunch (it might have stopped me if I had been in her place!). Her priority was to meet me and develop a friendship, not to impress me.

Margie *did* impress me, but not in the way the world desires to impress. I was impressed by her scriptural example of hospitality. She was not self-conscious about the simplicity of either her home or her lunch—there was not one word of apology. I doubt that it even occurred to her how differently I was being entertained than I had been on other job-hunting luncheons.

As we ate, Margie and I visited. It soon became evident that her hospitality was making an eternal difference in many lives. Not only was she hospitable to missionaries and those in ministry, but she had a thriving evangelistic study. More and more women from her block were coming, drawn to Margie, to her unintimidating and warm home, and to Jesus Christ, the center of it all.

Our study closes with a very personal letter, to Gaius, whom I believe exemplified many of the characteristics I saw in Margie. He loved to be hospitable to strangers for the sake of Jesus, and visitors to his home came back to John and remarked not on his impressive home but on his love.

WARMUP

Share a time when someone's hospitality particularly ministered to you. What was it that ministered to you?

Or, share who you think your secret sister is and why. Then have her reveal her identity.

DAY 1

The Beauty of Faithfulness

As in 2 John, John writes about the joy of finding "children" walking in the truth. Here he is referring to Gaius, who may have been one of his converts.

Memorize 3 John 5:

> *Dear friend, you are faithful in what you are doing for the brothers, even though they are strangers to you.*

Read through 3 John in its entirety, then read 3 John 1–6 again.

1. Find a way that John encourages Gaius in each of the six opening verses.

What were some of the outstanding evidences of Gaius's spiritual health?

On-the-Spot Action Assignment

Encourage one another in your small group by sharing some of the outstanding evidences of one another's spiritual health. Go around the group and allow a few sentences of encouragement for each woman.

What ordinary or creative ways can you think of to imitate John's habit of spiritually encouraging your sisters and brothers in Christ?

Review your memory passages from Weeks 1–3.

DAY 2

Christian Hospitality

The way the world entertains should be very different from the way a Christian extends hospitality. The world desires to impress, the Christian should desire to minister. The world exclusively invites those who will be able to repay; the Christian should be looking for ways, as Karen Mains says, "to be a catalyst for the miraculous."

2. As women, we are often the ones who decide whether or not and to whom our homes will be open. Here are just a few of the possibilities:

A. To encourage missionaries and ministry workers with a home-cooked meal and sharpening conversation.

B. To mentor younger women, helping them to love their husbands and children, inviting them into our homes and allowing them to see a model, as Titus 2 instructs.

C. To provide a warm and loving atmosphere for one-on-one evangelism or an evangelistic Bible study.

D. To provide a temporary home for a woman in need of nurturing.

E. To provide a temporary or permanent home to a foster child or orphan.

F. To welcome someone to the community.

3. What are some ways you have used your home in Christian hospitality? What dreams do you have for extending your practice of Christian hospitality?

Read 3 John 5–6.

4. To whom was Gaius showing hospitality?

A. Who do you know that would fit into this category?

B. What do you think verse 6 means?

C. What are some ways you could do this?

Read 3 John 7–8.

5. What did you learn about the recipients of Gaius' hospitality?

Why do you think they didn't receive help from unbelievers?

6. Read the following verses and write any added insight each gives you on Christian hospitality.

A. "Keep on loving each other as brothers. Do not forget to entertain strangers, for by so doing some people have entertained angels without knowing it" (Heb. 13:1–2).

B. "Then Jesus said to his host, 'When you give a luncheon or dinner, do not invite your friends, your brothers or relatives, or your rich neighbors; if you do, they may invite you back and so you will be repaid. But when you give a banquet, invite the poor, the crippled, the lame, the blind, and you will be blessed. Although they cannot repay you, you will be repaid at the resurrection of the righteous'" (Luke 14:12–14).

Action Assignment

Invite a newcomer, a missionary, a woman who could use mentoring, or someone else whom the Lord lays upon your heart, over for a meal or dessert. Make your invitation today for sometime in the next week. Share whom you invited and why.

Review your memory work from Weeks 4 and 5.

DAY 3

Be Hospitable to the Truth

In 2 John, we considered a broader application of the warning of being careful about welcoming anti-Christian propaganda into our homes by looking at mass media. Here in 3 John we see the positive side of this warning. We are encouraged to be hospitable to the truth. We women can increase our family's exposure to the truth through our guests and through the books, music, and programs we welcome into our homes.

7. If you were blessed to be raised in a home that was hospitable to the truth, share some ways your mother or father increased your exposure to the truth through:

A. Guests (Do you remember a particular missionary or Christian who had an impact on you?)

B. Music

C. Books

8. What can you do to make your home more hospitable to the truth?

9. What blessings did the following people receive by being hospitable to the truth?

A. The Shulammite woman (2 Kings 4:8–17)

B. The Philippian jailer (Acts 16:25–34)

What are some ways you or your family have been blessed by being hospitable to workers of the truth?

Virginia Hearns researched families of "well-turned-out" Christian children, looking for common variables. One commonality she found was that their homes were hospitable homes, frequently welcoming those who were in full-time Christian service. Their words and their lives helped the children of the host and hostess to grow immeasurably.

10. In Philippians 4:8, we're told to think about things that are true, noble, right, pure, lovely, admirable, excellent, and praiseworthy. List some specific books, radio programs, or movies that have helped you to do that. Share your list with your small group. (See Dee's list on her Web site: www.deebrestin.com.)

Review your memory work for weeks 6 and 7.

DAY 4

The Real Reason for Inhospitality

Scripture has the power to change lives if we are tender-hearted and willing to obey. Abbey is just such a woman. In response to my Bible study, *A Woman of Hospitality*, Abbey wrote:

> *I had the usual excuses for not practicing hospitality—my house wasn't nice enough, I wasn't a good enough cook, I didn't have enough money ... but your study stripped away my excuses and revealed the real reason for my inhospitality: a lack of concern for the needs of others. Scripture showed me that the heart of hospitality is showing love. When I started thinking about the needs of others and stopped worrying about how impressed they'd be with me or my house, I began to reach out. Now, these are the kind of things I'm doing regularly: having newcomers to the church over for popcorn on Sunday nights; picking up the son of a single mom when we go camping; and having our unsaved neighbors over for dessert while we draw them out with caring questions about their lives. These simple acts of obedience mean so much to them, and their joy wells up and makes our joy complete!*

Review 3 John 5–8, then read 3 John 9–10.

11. What three acts of inhospitality does John list about Diotrephes in this passage? According to verse 9, what was his motive?

12. What are typical reasons that people give for failing to welcome those who need welcoming? What tends to be the real reason for inhospitality?

13. Who are some people in your life who need welcoming? Who are some people in your life who fit John's description in verses 7–8?

A. When you think about the people in the above two categories, what, if anything, is keeping you from encouraging or welcoming them into your home?

B. How do you think God would have you overcome these obstacles?

Review your memory work for weeks 8 and 9.

DAY 5

Our Actions Reveal If God's Beauty Is in Us

John closes this letter with a familiar theme. If God really lives in you, you will do what is good. If your life is habitually evil (like the life of Diotrephes), then you have not seen God.

Read 3 John 11–13.

14. What does John say about Demetrius? How does he demonstrate one side of the principle in verse 11?

15. As a review of this principle, what point does John make in each of the following passages?

A. 1 John 1:5–6

B. 1 John 2:3–6

C. 1 John 2:9–11

D. 1 John 3:14–15

E. 1 John 3:16–20

F. 1 John 4:19–21

G. 2 John 9

16. List two specific truths that God has impressed upon your heart from the letters of John. How are these truths making a difference in your life? (Be specific.)

Recite this week's memory verse by heart.

PRAYER TIME

Use your answers to the last question as a guide for conversational prayer.

Leader's Helps

YOUR ROLE: A FACILITATOR FOR THE HOLY SPIRIT AND AN ENCOURAGER

A FACILITATOR FOR THE HOLY SPIRIT

People remember best what they articulate themselves, so your role is to encourage discussion and keep it on track. Here are some things you can do to help:

1. Ask questions and allow silence until someone speaks up. If the silence seems interminable, rephrase the question, but don't answer it yourself!

2. Direct the group members to look in Scripture for their answers. For example, ask, "How can you see John's excitement in verse 1?"

3. Place chairs in as small a circle as possible. Space inhibits sharing.

4. Deal with the monopolizer:

   A. Pray not only for her control, but that you can help find ways to make her feel valued. Excessive talking often springs from deep emotional needs.

   B. Wait for her to take a breath and gently say, "Thanks, could we hear from someone else?"

   C. Go around the room with a question.

   D. Take the monopolizer aside and say, "I value your input in the group. I have wondered if you realize how you come across at times." Though this is painful, it truly may help her to see herself and make changes that will help her dramatically.

5. The Action Assignments and memory work will be useful in your group members' lives. If they aren't doing these exercises, call a few from the group and ask them to be good examples with you. Soon the others will follow!

6. Occasionally call on the shy people when it seems they might have something to share but need a little encouragement. Tell them they can simply toss the ball to someone else by saying, "I don't know, Linda, what do you think?" if they don't have anything to share. If they form this habit in the beginning, you will have a richly interactive group instead of just hearing from the few who are comfortable sharing.

7. Bring name tags the first few weeks and put first names in large letters with a black marker.

8. If your group has trouble getting through all the questions, circle the questions you want to discuss in the group and pace yourself.

AN ENCOURAGER

Most women who drop out of a group do so not because the study is too challenging, but because they don't feel valued. As a leader, these are some of the things you can do to help each woman feel valued:

1. Greet each woman warmly when she walks in the door. This meeting should be the high point of her week!

2. Affirm answers when you can genuinely do so: "Good insight! Great! Thank you!" And always affirm nonverbally with your eyes, a smile, and a nod.

3. If a woman gives a wrong or off-the-wall answer, be careful not to crush her. You can still affirm her by saying, "That's interesting, what does someone else think?" If you feel her response must be corrected, someone in the group will probably do it. If they don't, space your correction so it doesn't immediately follow her response and is not obviously directed at her.

4. If this is an interdenominational group, set the ground rule that no one is to speak unfavorably of another denomination.

5. Send notes to absentees and postcards in appreciation to the faithful. Collect email addresses, for this will simplify your role immensely.

6. Don't skimp on the prayer time. Women's emotional and spiritual needs are met during the prayer time. If they can learn to lift their needs directly in prayer, it will not take a lot of time.

Leader's Helps for A Woman of Beauty

ONE
What Makes a Woman Beautiful?

This lesson may need to be divided, especially if they have not gotten their guides ahead of time. In that case, go as far as you can and assign the rest of the lesson for the next week.

1. Note the expansive descriptions of his power in the opening verses and the almost blasphemous phrase in verse 4. Note the ostentatious display in verses 5–8. Note how seven eunuchs with comical-sounding names were needed to bring one woman. Note the edict that was supposed to inspire respect!

2. The men had been drinking as much as they desired for seven days. This was like asking Vashti to pop out of a cardboard cake. Some historians, such as Josephus, claim she was asked to appear in the nude. Whether or not they are correct, it was clear it was a demeaning and dangerous request.

6. A concubine is not a virgin, but a woman who gives a man all the privileges of marriage yet receives no honor or protection in return.

8. Some say this description only referred to Jesus on the cross, but there are other indications that Jesus may not have been physically beautiful. There is great surprise that this carpenter from Nazareth could be anyone of importance (Matt. 13:54–56), and the Pharisees seemed to think He looked older than He was (John 8:57).

16C. In Christ, though our sins are as scarlet, they are made as white as snow.

TWO
Beautiful Beyond Description

5. God spoke the world into being, using words to create all things.

6. Jesus is the way God communicates with man (see Heb. 1:1).

7. Jesus became flesh when the Spirit overshadowed Mary and formed in her womb. The disciples beheld His glory many times, but John may be recalling the glory of the transfiguration or the ascension.

21. This question could be difficult for beginners, and you may need to lead the way or call upon more mature believers to articulate a time when they were consoled by

118

Christ, felt a kindred spirit with another and realized it was because she knew Christ, or felt affection for someone because of Jesus, etc.

24. This is your opportunity to encourage group members to keep standards high: have their homework and memory work done, share honestly and vulnerably, keep confidences, and pray for one another.

THREE
A Woman of Beauty Walks in the Light

9A. Walking in the light as He is in the light always works; whereas, sometimes we cannot or should not do what Jesus would do. Christ alone has a holy prerogative, for example, to show His wrath or to be jealous for us with a godly jealousy.

FOUR
A Woman of Beauty Walks in Love

1C. You may need to pave the way by making yourself vulnerable first.

8B. It is like it, but narrower, to love the family of God. We are not to forsake love for our neighbor, but the world should be able to see a genuine affection and harmony between members in the family of God.

13. It is new in that it is narrower, loving within the family of God, and yet loving others is as old as the commands given through Moses. It has also been seen more clearly through the life of Christ.

22. Just as Solomon was attracted to the Shulammite maiden because of her physical charms, so the world may be attracted or repelled by the outside appearance of Christians.

FIVE
A Woman of Beauty Walks in Truth

2. Jesus means "savior" and Christ means "anointed one." Jesus came to save His people from their sins, and He is the One, and the only One, God anointed for this purpose (see 1 John 2:22 and John 14:1–2). He is fully God (John 1:1–3; Col. 1:19).

5. All of the images have various kinds of spiritual adultery in common. Instead of trusting in God and in His pure message, they are running to false gods and believing teachers who have twisted the purity of the message.

6D. We cannot become mature if we must rely on "bottle feeding," on having someone else feed us.

SIX
The Distinctive Beauty of Calvary Love

11E. When we hate the child, we simultaneously show hatred toward the parent. We are one with God. When Saul was persecuting Christians, Jesus said, "Saul, Saul, why do you persecute me?" (Acts 9:4).

18D. It is counterfeit, just like an artificial tree. There is no life in it.

SEVEN
The Beauty of Overcoming Love

2B. Not being open and not listening is not the only test, but it is a red flag. Another red flag is when the teaching is warmly embraced by those in the world.

EIGHT
The Woman of Beauty Is Confident

9. We cannot expect to receive when we pray apart from His will, for He always does what is best for us. He may at times give us what we want to discipline us, as He gave the Israelites a king when they preferred that over trusting Him. 1 John 3:22 doesn't mean we can arm wrestle God into giving us what we want, for He is sovereign and will give us what is best. But if our hearts are pure, and that purity is reflected by right living, we are more likely to be in His will and to be asking for things within His will.

NINE
The Beauty Is Passed On

12. Though we want to be wary of legalism, there are some who have limited television successfully without being legalistic. If someone in your group has done so in a spirit of humility, ask her to share a few sentences.

Plan a coffee or extended time with a meal for your last session. You'll be revealing secret sisters.

TEN
The Beauty of Hospitality

4. Sending missionaries out in a manner worthy of the gospel means filling their cups—not only with material blessings, but also with encouragement, prayer, and love.

Memory Verses

Chapter 1
This is the message we have heard from him and declare to you: God is light; in him there is no darkness at all. (1 John 1:5)

Chapter 2
If we claim to have fellowship with him yet walk in the darkness, we lie and do not live by the truth. (1 John 1:6)

Chapter 3
But if we walk in the light, as he is in the light, we have fellowship with one another, and the blood of Jesus, his Son, purifies us from all sin. (1 John 1:7)

Chapter 4
Beloved, let us love one another: for love is of God; and every one that loveth is born of God, and knoweth God. He that loveth not knoweth not God; for God is love. (1 John 4:7–8 KJV)

Chapter 5
Who is the liar? It is the man who denies that Jesus is the Christ. Such a man is the antichrist—he denies the Father and the Son. (1 John 2:22)

Chapter 6
This is how we know what love is: Jesus Christ laid down his life for us. And we ought to lay down our lives for our brothers. (1 John 3:16)

Chapter 7
Ye are of God, little children, and have overcome them: because greater is he that is in you, than he that is in the world. (1 John 4:4 KJV)

Chapter 8
I write these things to you who believe in the name of the Son of God so that you may know that you have eternal life. (1 John 5:13)

Chapter 9
Anyone who runs ahead and does not continue in the teaching of Christ does not have God; whoever continues in the teaching has both the Father and the Son. (2 John 9)

Chapter 10
Dear friend, you are faithful in what you are doing for the brothers, even though they are strangers to you. (3 John 5)

Hymns Index

Holy Is The Lord

Lyrics by Chris Tomlin

We stand and lift up our hands
For the joy of the Lord is our strength
We bow down and worship Him now
How great, how awesome is He

And together we sing
Everyone sing

Holy is the Lord God Almighty
The earth is filled with His glory
Holy is the Lord God Almighty
The earth is filled with His glory
The earth is filled with His glory

We stand and lift up our hands
For the joy of the Lord is our strength
We bow down and worship Him now
How great, how awesome is He

And together we sing
Everyone sing

Holy is the Lord God Almighty
The earth is filled with His glory
Holy is the Lord God Almighty
The earth is filled with His glory
The earth is filled with His glory

It's rising up all around
It's the anthem of the Lord's renown

Beloved (1 John 4:7-8)

Dennis Ryder

This Is My Commandment

Author Unknown

If We Walk in the Light

Author Unknown

If we walk in the light as He is in the light,

we have fel-low-ship one with an-oth-er. Then the

blood of Je-sus Christ, it clean-ses ev-'ry sin, if we

walk in the light as He is in the light. And the

light from with-in can shine on ev-'ry heart, so now

let your light shine, to ev-'ry-one im-part. If we

Behold, What Manner of Love

I John 3:1

Patricia Van Tine

5 Fairest Lord Jesus

FROM THE GERMAN 17TH CENTURY
4TH VERSE TR. JOSEPH A. SEISS

SILESIAN FOLK SONG
ARR. BY RICHARD S. WILLIS

1. Fair - est Lord Je - sus! Ru - ler of all na - ture!
2. Fair are the mead - ows, Fair - er still the wood - lands,
3. Fair is the sun - shine, Fair - er still the moon - light,
4. Beau - ti - ful Sav - ior! Lord of all the na - tions!

O Thou of God and man the Son! Thee will I cher - ish,
Robed in the bloom - ing garb of spring; Je - sus is fair - er,
And all the twin - kling star - ry host; Je - sus shines bright - er,
Son of God and Son of Man! Glo - ry and hon - or,

Thee will I hon - or, Thou, my soul's glo - ry, joy, and crown!
Je - sus is pur - er, Who makes the woe - ful heart to sing!
Je - sus shines pur - er, Than all the an - gels heav'n can boast!
Praise, a - dor - a - tion, Now and for - ev - er - more be Thine! A - MEN.

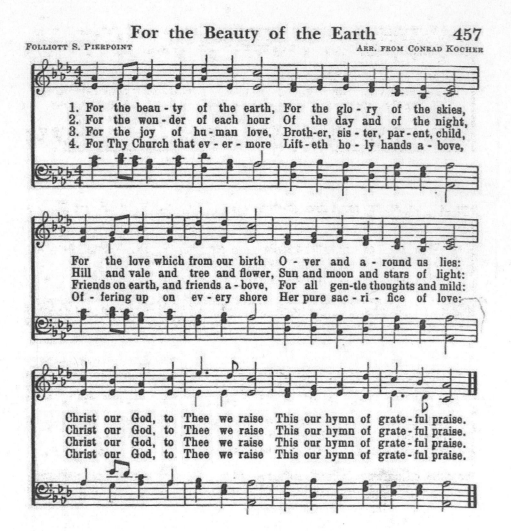

For the Beauty of the Earth 457

Folliott S. Pierpoint   Arr. from Conrad Kocher

1. For the beau-ty of the earth, For the glo-ry of the skies,
2. For the won-der of each hour Of the day and of the night,
3. For the joy of hu-man love, Broth-er, sis-ter, par-ent, child,
4. For Thy Church that ev-er-more Lift-eth ho-ly hands a-bove,

For the love which from our birth O-ver and a-round us lies:
Hill and vale and tree and flower, Sun and moon and stars of light:
Friends on earth, and friends a-bove, For all gen-tle thoughts and mild:
Of-fering up on ev-ery shore Her pure sac-ri-fice of love:

Christ our God, to Thee we raise This our hymn of grate-ful praise.
Christ our God, to Thee we raise This our hymn of grate-ful praise.
Christ our God, to Thee we raise This our hymn of grate-ful praise.
Christ our God, to Thee we raise This our hymn of grate-ful praise.